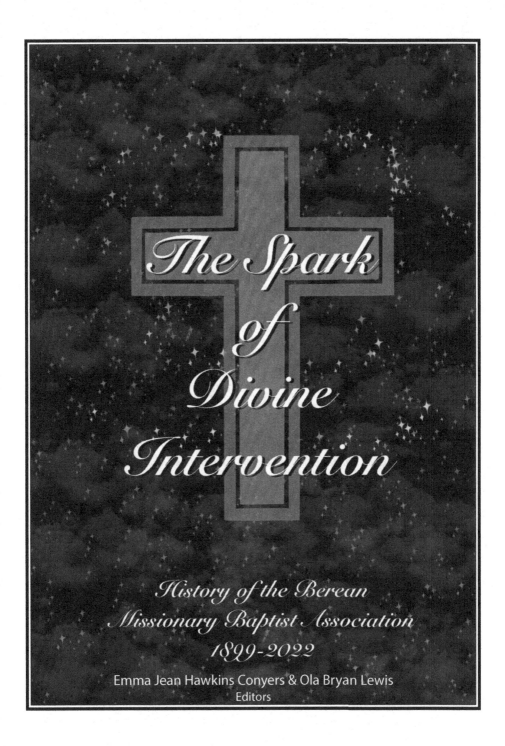

The Spark
of
Divine
Intervention

History of the Berean Missionary Baptist Association 1899-2022

Emma Jean Hawkins Conyers & Ola Bryan Lewis
Editors

THE SPARK OF DIVINE INTERVENTION
HISTORY OF THE BEREAN MISSIONARY
BAPTIST ASSOCIATION 1899 - 2022

iUniverse books may be ordered through booksellers or by contacting:

iUniverse
1663 Liberty Drive
Bloomington, IN 47403
www.iuniverse.com
844-349-9409

ISBN: 978-1-6632-5912-7 (sc)
ISBN: 978-1-6632-5913-4 (e)

Library of Congress Control Number: 2023924233

Print information available on the last page.

iUniverse rev. date: 01/23/2024

History of the Berean Missionary Baptist Association

In
Memory
Sis. Ivy Dianne Page Richardson

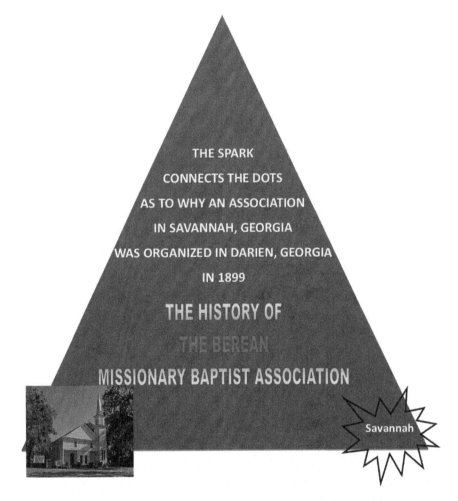

THE SPARK

CONNECTS THE DOTS

AS TO WHY AN ASSOCIATION

IN SAVANNAH, GEORGIA

WAS ORGANIZED IN DARIEN, GEORGIA

IN 1899

THE HISTORY OF

THE BEREAN

MISSIONARY BAPTIST ASSOCIATION

Savannah

Part I Written by:
Mrs. Ivy D. Richardson

The Berean Missionary Baptist Association

History Committee 2022 -2023, Part II

Sis. Emma Jean Hawkins Conyers, Editor

Sis. Ola Bryan Lewis, Co-Editor

Contributors

Sis. Evelyn Green

Sis. Willie Hall, *Savannah Tribune* Researcher

Sis. Patricia Henderson

Sis. Kathy Morgan

Sis. Florrie Scriven

Sis. Carolyn B. Scott

Sis. Gwendolyn P. Sheppard

Sis. Diana Wagner, *Savannah Tribune* Researcher

Sis. Thomasina White

Rev. Clarence Williams

Moderator Andre J. Osborne, Ex Officio

Contents

Moderators

Rev. P. J. Butler, 1899 – unknown period served

Rev. W. L. P. Weston – unknown period served

Rev. William S. Gray, 1918 – 1942

Rev. Eddie Daniel Davis, 1943 – 1944

Rev. S. A. Baker, 1945 – 1948

Rev. Eugene Aiken Capers, 1949- 1982

Rev. William Daniels, 1983-1999

Rev. Matthew Southall Brown, Sr., 2000 – 2012

Rev. Clarence Williams, Jr. 2013-2019

Rev. Richard L. Hall, Sr. 2019 – 2020

Rev. Andre Osborne 2021 – present

Foreword

"Jesus said to her, 'I am the resurrection and the life. Those who believe in me, even though they die, will live, and everyone who lives and believes in me will never die.'" Sis. Ivy Dianne Page Richardson lives not only with Christ but also with the Bereans today. She was called from labor to reward June 27, 2018, leaving her earthly assignment incomplete to be completed by those who hear her charge, "to serve the present age in real time."

Moderator Clarence Williams asked the service of Sis. Ola B. Lewis and me to complete Ivy's earthly assignment. We accepted Moderator Williams's request. We were introduced to the Berean body as the succeeding writers and began to serve in this honored position. We wanted to do Sis. Richardson justice in her writing since we both loved and adored her. Ivy was a member of Sis. Lewis's church, Tremont Temple Missionary Baptist Church, and she was a member of my sorority, Alpha Kappa Alpha Sorority, Inc., Gamma Sigma Omega Chapter. Although the willingness to complete the task was heart driven, the task, due to so many unknown ideas in her document, was mind troubling, questions that we couldn't answer, and we lacked committee members who were knowledgeable about the Berean Association from whom we could ask assistance. This void made writing problematic for Sis. Lewis and me. Many times, we were left wringing our hands and wondering what to do next. I expressed to Sis. Lewis, "Why is she talking so much about Darien, Georgia? I guess I will have to go to Darien to find answers." But God said, "Wait a minute." Rev. Clarence Williams resigned as Moderator of the Berean Association, 2019. With his resignation, Sis. Lewis and I stopped completing the history started by Sis. Richardson.

However, in June 2022, I attended the Associations' meeting of the General Missionary Baptist Convention of GA, Inc. The State Women's Auxiliary Leader, Sis. Ruthie P. Lewis, encouraged the Associations to write their histories. She asked how many Associations had written histories. Only a few responded affirmatively. Yes, I became convicted to complete Sis. Richardson's Berean Missionary Baptist Association History. I could hear her words, "to serve the present age in real time."

"All things work for good for those who love the Lord and called to His purpose." The very next morning after that General Missionary Baptist Convention Association meeting, going into vote early, I ran into Sis. Ola B. Lewis. We had not seen each other in over two years. Our meeting was confirmation for me that I must "serve this present age in real time." I asked her would she be willing to continue the writing, and she agreed.

I then called Sis. Evelyn Green, President of the Women's Auxiliary of the Berean Association. Sis. Green offered her support and promised to contact the Moderator, Rev. Andre Osborne, for his approval. He granted it. Sis. Green and I agreed for the committee to meet in September 2022 to plan for the writing of history. This time, a committee knowledgeable about the Berean Association was formed with Sis. Ola B. Lewis and me at the helm.

This book is divided into two parts: The Story Unfolds, Part I, is Ivy Richardson's writing of the Berean Missionary Baptist Association's history. Churches that responded to Sis. Richardson's request appear prior to her conclusion. Churches that responded to this committee's request appear prior to Epilogue in Part II. Also, the write up on Dean Betty West is an addition to Part I due to Sis. Richardson's omission of Dean West's information. Part II is this committee's research that contains insightful, clarification, and additional information, 1899 – 2023.

Sis. Richardson invoked questions that we know this book will answer: "Why would a Savannah based organization have its initial meeting in Darien, Georgia? Why the name Berean? How did the nation's history impact the organization? And how the organization evolved to what it is one hundred seventeen [123] years later?"

Sis. Emma Jean Conyers

Part I

[Part I]

Introduction

Dreams are visions of that which should be; a vision gives insight as to how a dream should look; goals give directions as to how a dream should become; and objectives give guiding statements on the strategies for implementation. This book renders the reality of our forefathers' dream as now revealed to the imagination of your mind. You will see God's guiding hand upon this organization through its name, its leaders, its workers, and its impact upon the community. The untold story reveals a spiritual spark that began on the Damascus Road and transcended through time to a little city in the deep south of Georgia, penetrated throughout that state, and continues to ignite the Savannah's faith-based community. This book encompasses the reality of the organization's existence based on its membership of one body.

You will see God's hand in the selection and preparation of Pastors to serve as Moderators, and you will read about the impact on the lives of children who grew up in the Association and took on

1

leadership roles. You will see preparation linked to those serving as Moderators, Deans for the Congress of Christian Education, and Deans of Christian Leadership Schools. Look at your church's role in God's preparation for the Association. But in all your reading, get understanding about the longevity of the organization.

The present day community is made aware of the Berean Missionary Baptist Association Incorporated's annual and weekly activities or events, as posted in the local media. The media includes the *Savannah Morning News*; and the two local papers generated throughout the black community: the *Savannah Herald* and the *Savannah Tribune*. Yet, there is no reflection of the organization's evolvement in a bound copy for future generations to reflect on the past, to deal with the present, and to impact the future. Nor in this age of technology, can one research the impact of the Black Baptist Missionary Churches coming together as one Association to serve the Savannah community. This book gives a reflection of the Biblical impact in the development of this organization while America's history impacted the needs and structure of the organization. This book is evidence of a group of dedicated and determined workers' commitment to assure what your hands hold, your eyes read, your imagination reveals, your ears hear, as the book enhances your knowledge base, and serves as a point of historical reference about Savannah's faith based Black Missionary Baptist community.

Moderator, Rev. Matthew Southall Brown, Sr., knew there would be a need to "know" about the spark that transitioned from the Damascus Road into Darien, Georgia. A spark that continued to burn for over one hundred seventeen years (117) in the Savannah community. Moderator Brown's dream of how one could address an untold story and assure a resource for generations to come became an objective during his administration. Moderator Matthew Southall Brown, Sr. appointed a committee to collect artifacts and write the history of the Association in 2002. The committee was composed of Dea. Johnnie P. Jones, Sr. of Mt. Zion Missionary Baptist Church, Sis. Carrie L. Rouse, Jerusalem Missionary Baptist Church, Sis. Parnell M. Jones, Mt Zion Missionary Baptist Church, and Rev. Larry J. Stell, Pastor of Central Missionary Baptist Church of Hitch Village. Sis. Verlene Lamply volunteered to assist the committee but dropped out because of her workload. Dea. Jones kept scrapbooks of the materials and a written history on the organization of the Association until his death February 27, 2013. Those scrapbooks are now in his son's possession.

His wife, Sis. Parnell M. Jones did not want the Committee's labor to be in vain; therefore, she called upon this writer in the spring of 2013 to take on the task of completing the history of the Association. This writer began in prayer and the words of a song written by Charles Wesley in 1762 came to mind, "A Charge to keep

3

I have, a God to glorify, a never dying soul to save, and fit it for the sky. To serve the present age, my calling to fulfill; Oh, may it all my powers engage to do my Master's will!" It is God's will that I complete this untold story to ***include the historical development of the churches within the Association.***

In July of 2013, Sis. Parnell Jones was presented with a five-page draft of this document. The initial document contained information about the organizational meeting, the name of the Moderators, and records of the Annual Sessions. Yet, it does not address, "Why would a Savannah based organization have its initial meeting in Darien, Georgia? Why the name Berean? How did the nation's history impact the organization? And how the organization evolved to what it is one hundred seventeen years later?" So, as you turn the pages in real time, read about the spark that ignited this writer's desire to expand beyond the five pages read by Sis. Parnell Jones. You will see God's hand of time revealed in the life of the Association's workers. May it ignite you, the reader, the future Moderators, Deans, and Congress workers to fulfill your call to serve the present age in real time. But above all, may it motivate you, the Clerk and Historian, to preserve all records by filing the minutes in Mercer University's Historical Baptist Depository.

Sis. Ivy Dianne Page Richardson

DEDICATED TO

"The Committee's labor is not in vain as you gaze your eyes upon the pages of this book. Please keep in mind that the recording of this history would not be possible had it not been for the presence of those Christian men at the First African Baptist Church of Darien, Georgia. We give thanks for the Pastors, members, and those who contributed to the development and service of this outstanding association, TO GOD BE THE GLORY..." These words were so eloquently penned by the Historian and History Committee's Chairperson of the Berean Missionary Baptist Association, Dea. Johnnie P. Jones. Dea. Jones was a member of Mt. Zion Missionary Baptist Church in Savannah, Georgia. Thank you Dea. Jones for being a keeper of the organization's records.

Dea. Johnnie P. Jones,
Historian of the Berean Missionary Baptist
Association 2002- 2013

The committee began the vision of the seventh [eighth] Moderator, Matthew Southall Brown, Sr. in the year of 2002. Thank you, Pastor Brown for the assignment to understand why those Pastors organized the Association in Darien, Georgia. Fifteen years ago, your dream and vision became the Committee's objectives. Four years ago, this writer took up the spark and goal to assure your vision is now a reality, the reality of a tool for future generations to understand the question, "Why Darien, Georgia?"

Dean Betty West

Dean Betty J. West was educated in the local schools of Savannah, Georgia. She is a 1962 Sol C. Johnson High School honor graduate. She matriculated at Savannah State College (now University) and received her B.S. degree in Mathematics Education and a minor in Science. She taught for 33 years in the local schools with 3 years at Mercer Middle School, 30 years at Shuman Middle School, and two years in Adult Education at Savannah Vocational Technical School (now Savannah Technical College). She retired in June 2000.

She is a member of Second Arnold Baptist Church with over 50 years of membership. She has worked in various organizations in the church: First Director of Vacation Bible School, past secretary of the Sunday School, Sunday School Teacher of Adult Women's class, Usher, Co-Chairperson of Christian Education, Chairperson of committee to form the George Dingle Scholarship, member of the Deaconess Ministry, Sunday School, Berean Women's Auxiliary, and Board member of Bryant Theological Bible College (GMBC). She has been Dean of the Local Congress for the past 21 plus years and is a national certified Dean (for 26 years). As a worker in Christ's Army, Sis. West was Director of the first Christian Leadership School of Second Arnold Church in 1999, where Dea. Robert Lee West was Dean. Dea. West and Sis. West started "The West Team Ministry" in 1997 as Christian Education Consultants. They are two certified Deans of Christian Education, teaching, training, and working with other Baptist Churches and groups, such as promoting the Sunday School Publishing Board's December Conference for the Certificate of Progress Program (COPP) certificate/diploma and church Growth-Helpers of Christ.

She is a founding member of the National Deans and Presidents Alumni Association which was organized in Nashville, Tennessee in the SSPB Conference for over 10 years.

She is the First Director/Dean of the Berean Congress – 38th Annual Session to monitor Sis. Cynthia E. Fearbry (Mikell) into Certified Deanship (Green, "Betty West Bio").

A SPARK OF DIVINE INTERVENTION
ON
MARKET STREET

MARKET STREET OF DARIEN, GEORGIA
A street of Insurrection-Civil Disobedience-Civil Rights Meetings

The backdoors of this jailhouse on Market Street
face the front doors of the **oldest** African American
Church in Darien, Georgia.

The Spark

Dea. Johnnie P. Jones pens the history with, "A fire was ignited in 1899 by several Christian men and has not ceased to burn through the past one hundred plus years. The Berean Missionary Baptist Association of Georgia was organized in July of 1899 by a group of spiritual men, the late Rev. William Gray, Rev. J.J. Dunham, S. Buford, R. H. Thompson, and others in Darien, Georgia at the First African Baptist Church. The first Moderator was Rev. P. J. Butler. Some of the churches present were First Bryan Baptist, Saint John Baptist, First Tabernacle Baptist, Happy Home Baptist, Bethlehem Baptist, and others from Savannah, Georgia; First African Baptist and Grace Baptist of Darien, Georgia; White Oak Baptist of Montieth, Georgia; Elm Grove Baptist of Meridan, Georgia; Abyssinia Baptist of Brunswick, Georgia, and other churches yet to be identified."

Robert Garner (2012) writes that prior to freedom, the African Americans were forced to join the white dominated church. But in 1865, "the Zion Baptist Association was formed in the state, followed by Ebenezer Missionary Baptist Association." Wagner (1980) gives more clarity to Zion's location that was located across the river on Hilton Head Island. The year 1865 may come to mind, for it was on December 6, 1865 that the states ratified the Thirteenth Amendment, the amendment that eliminated slavery. Yet, there are still no records to indicate why thirty-four years later, the spiritual men met on July of 1899 in Darien, Georgia.

However, the resources of today's technology give insight on the state of the nation in 1899. A review of the National Advancement for Colored People's document of lynching in the United States shows that of the sixty-five (65) lynchings in 1899, only twenty-six (26) took place in the state of Georgia. The report lists every county or city in Georgia where mobs and lynchings took place; however, the literary review reveals no listing of Savannah, Brunswick, Monteith, Meridian, or Darien. Yet, the literary review noticed the rumors of a possible lynching to take place in August 1899 in Darien, Georgia. One month later, the spark was ignited in the organizational meeting of the Association in the oldest church of Darien.

Ida B. Wells (1899) wrote on Lynching Laws and the protection of Negroes from lynching by orders of Governor William Yates Atkinson. She writes about the lynching of a Negroe [Negro] preacher name Sam Hose, in Palmetto, Georgia in April of 1899. She noted that the governor had notified the law enforcement agency to move Hose to Atlanta, Georgia for safe keeping. However, she found that the agency made no effort to stop the lynching, and so she employed an individual investigator to investigate the event. The investigator reported, "The event was advertised and subsequently, a few thousand men, women, and children showed up for the spectacle, and the lynching was duly executed in a carnival like atmosphere, where attendants clamored for fragments of Hose's remains.

13

The investigation in Georgia concluded with the exposure of the lawlessness of sheriffs and police officers, whose fidelity was to their local community rather than their sworn duties and in deference to the mandates of the executive branch of the state." Rev. Hose was guilty of killing his boss after the boss attacked him, but he was tried by the mob, not by a jury.

Ida B. Wells writes of the Lynch Laws, safe keeping, and relocation, but a review of the literature, reports that Governor Atkinson's death was August 8, 1899. The literary review noted the "rumors" of a possible lynching to take place in August of 1899 in Darien, Georgia, in the new jail house built across the street from the oldest African American church on Market Street. The stage is set as the story unfolds when the African American male was persecuted for insulting or raping a white female. The crime was more severe than murder, and mobs would overtake the jailhouse, lynch the man, mutilate the body, draw lots for the body parts, and leave them on display for public view. The city of Darien, Georgia's website confirms the Old Jail Art building as one of its three oldest public buildings. Although it is an art museum now, the cells and instructions for locking the doors are still posted with items on display (see pictures on the website). The website also cites, the First African Baptist Church as the oldest church in the county. The church was built in 1834 but was destroyed during the Civil War. The present building is a replica built in 1868. One key observation on the website is that not only has the oldest church withstood the weathering of time, but it also served as a meeting site for ***Civil Rights meetings and has a bell tower*** to summon attendees.

The church and the jailhouse as shown in the picture have more in common than "Market Street". First, the county built the jailhouse on Market Street diagonal to the church a year before the rumor had spread. Thus, the back door of the jailhouse faces the front door of the church and remains that way today because both are historical markers. The fire escape to the second floor led to the cells, which housed all prisoners; the officers' quarters were downstairs. A second factor is the jail housed a well-known Negroe [Negro] citizen of Darien, who was about to be denied the right to "Due Process" and put to death had the white mob convicted him of the worst crime committed by an African American male. Note that this writer's usage of the term, "Mob" not "Jury". The third factor is the church's bell tower.

The stairs of the church led to a place for Civil Rights meetings. The bell had to ring and give understanding why there were representatives in Darien, Georgia from the cities of Savannah and Brunswick, along with the county of Effingham at First African Baptist Church on Market Street in Darien, Georgia. Read the article below with its grammatical flaws.

"Saturday 26 August 1899"

Pg. 3 col. 3

WEDNESDAY'S DISGRACE

A mob of several hundred negroes took charge of McIntosh County jail on Wednesday morning last and prevented the sheriff from conveying **Henry Delegal**, a negro charged with capital offense, to the Savannah jail for safe keeping. The sheriff intended carrying **Delegal** off on the 10:20 train but the presence of the well-armed mob deterred him from doing so. It was humiliating beyond measure to the law-abiding citizens of Darien. But as the lawless proceedings were altogether unexpected of course they were not prepared for the emergency [sic]. The governor was telegraphed for troops, and at 7 in the afternoon 200 troops from Savannah, under command of **Captain Gleason**, reached Darien. On arrival, they proceeded at once to the jail. The crowd of negroes were dispersed and the prisoner was carried to the train and sent to Savannah, most of the troops going back. **Captain Grayson**, with about 60 men" remained here to preserve order. During the day and up to the time of the arrival of the troops, the negroes were absolutely in charge of the jail, without authority and in defiance of law. It was the intention of THE GAZETTE to give the **Delegal** matter a passing notice and nothing more but the bad negroes of the county have taken the matter out of our hands and they will now have to suffer the consequences. We have often praised them as law-abiding and good citizens, and it is now with a feeling of sorrow that we are compelled to publish their outrageous proceedings of Wednesday last. They can blame no one [sic] but themselves and the disgrace now reals [sic] with them.

Many arrests have been made and we understand that a special term will be called for next week to try the law-breakers. As we go to press everything is quiet again.

Col. A.R. Lawton came down from Savannah on Thursday night to look over the situation. He came here at the request of **Gov. Candler.**

The September 1, 1899 edition of the *Atlanta Journal's* story links the prison to the church and to the cities. The special editorial speaks to the population of Darien, the political attributes of the Negroe [Negro], the influential status of the Negroe [Negro], the collaboration by the Negroe [Negro], and the transition from being identified as African American to now being called, "the Negroe [Negro]". The Negroes of McIntosh County outnumbered the whites four to one, controlled the vote, and the offices of Postmaster and Deputy Collector of Customs. The article describes Henry Denegal [Delegal] as a very influential powerful Negroe [Negro] who had a good relationship with the whites in Darien, Georgia. He became a Republican leader, moved into a dense swamp, and became ruler over the area in which he resided. However, the swamp property was surrounded by poor Whites who claimed to fear Henry's power. Living in the area was a white woman described as poor in character who became pregnant by Henry. It was after the birth of her mulatto daughter, that the woman reported Henry raped her on December 2, 1898. This was the greatest crime committed by a "colored"; and the rumors began.

Benjamin Brawley writes of a rumor that was stirring for days throughout the region about a possible lynching for raping a white girl. Valencia King Nelson confirms the rumor as she writes, "HENRY DELEGAL was a Darien black accused of raping a white girl in 1899. Fear that he would be lynched brought out a protective force of McIntosh blacks." Malcolm Bell, Jr. confirms this writer's thoughts on the ***spiritual spark*** as he records the following statement on the rumor and actions of the McIntosh County's citizens. "Henry Delegal was a Darien Black accused of raping a white girl in 1899. Fear that he would be lynched brought out a force of McIntosh Blacks, many of whom were from the Butler slaves' stock. Jailed in the disturbance that followed were Renty Young, Simon Devereataux, Andrew Young, John and Richard Coffee, Marshall Dowse, and William and Jack Cooper. The Reverend F.M. Mann of St. Cyprian's Church telegraphed Sarah Wister for help. She called the honored names of Channing, Curtis, Furmess, Garrison, Higginson, Lowell, Mort, and Shaw, all of whom sent money for a **spirited** defense that won Henry Delegal's acquittal and limited a chain gang sentence for the rioters."

Brawley goes on to say, "Violence breeds violence, and two or three outstanding events are yet to be recorded. On August 23, 1899, at Darien, Georgia, hundreds of Negroes, who for days had been aroused by rumors of a threatened lynching, assembled at the ringing of the bell of a church opposite the jail, and their presence prevented the removal of a prisoner. They were later tried for insurrection, and twenty-one prisoners were sent to the convict farms for a year. The general circumstances of the uprising excited great interest throughout the country." The other outstanding event includes the arrest of Denegal's [Delegal's] family in the killing of Darien's sheriff.

The *Atlanta Journal's* article, dated September 1899, identified a group of preachers who went into the swamp of Darien. Their purpose was to meet with Denegal's [Delegal's] family and the Insurrection of Disobedience participants. They encouraged them to surrender to the soldiers for protection and guaranteed a fair trial by an impartial jury. The most significant concept that evolved from the article is the identification of the group of preachers' publications. The article goes on to state that the group of preachers and other intelligent leaders gave credit to the soldiers for keeping Henry safe from the lynching mob and all other participants in their first circular (newspaper or newsletter).

The bell of the First African Church had to ring on August 23, 1899 to assure the safety of the prisoner from the lynching mob. The bell had to ring for the twenty-one plus rioters to put their trust in the United States' Volunteer Soldiers. The bell had to ring for all three sets of prisoners to have a military escort to the jail in Savannah. The bell had to ring for each prisoner to have a change of venue from the courtrooms of Darien, Georgia to either Effingham County or the city of Brunswick. The bell had to ring so Henry Denegal [Delegal] could give God thanks for the safety of his family as he observed them being escorted to jail by the U.S.V. (United States Volunteers) in Savannah, Georgia. The bell had to ring during the first Moderator's, Rev. P.J. Butler's tenure.

The bell identifies why the organizational meeting took place in First African of Darien, Georgia and not Grace Baptist of Darien. Grace Baptist could not observe the Jail House nor was there a bell to ring. The bell explains why members of the Savannah faith-based community traveled to an organizational meeting so that the prisoners would be housed under the safe protection of the soldiers stationed in Savannah. The bell reveals the role of Brunswick, Guyton, and Effingham as places of fair trials. The bell had to ring for the actions performed by the group of preachers' encouragements, resulted in the assurance of Henry Denegal [Delegal], his wife, their sons, and the rioters' guarantee of their right to "Due Process" (fair procedures). Henry and his wife were acquitted; their sons received life in prison; and the rioters either spent a year on the chain gang or paid a fine. Yet, no one was degraded, put on display, or their body parts sold for lots. We give thanks to the group of preachers for their first publication in September of 1899. Should anyone think it was by chance that the circular was published two months after the Berean Missionary Baptist Association's members met at the church where the bell had to ring?

The bell was donated by another influential Negroe [Negro] and his wife on November 8, 1887(FAB's History). The years are in layers of three as we view the chronological order of the bell, the jailhouse, and the acquittal. May the reader's mind reveal God's plans for the Association as Henry Todd donated a bell that saved another Henry's life. This History is important to each one who reads and comprehends God's divine purpose in the development of the Berean Missionary Baptist Association Incorporated, the development of churches within the Association, and the leadership to fulfill His divine will for longevity of the Association.

DIVINE INTERVENTION
IN THE NAME

"[3] And as he journeyed, he came near Damascus: and suddenly there shined round about him a light from heaven:

[4] And he fell to the earth, and heard a voice saying unto him, Saul, Saul, why persecutest thou me?

[5] And he said, who art thou, Lord? And the Lord said, I am Jesus whom thou persecutest: it is hard for thee to kick against the pricks.

[6] And he trembling and astonished said, Lord, what wilt thou have me to do? And the Lord said unto him, Arise, and go into the city, and it shall be told thee what thou must do." Acts 9:3-6KJV

"The Spark – The Great Commission"

We all know the story of Saul's request to the High Priest, that he rid the synagogues in Damascus of those who served Jesus. He was granted that wish, but there was an encounter on the Damascus Road that led to Saul's conversion. Saul met Jesus the Christ for himself when a sparkle of light from heaven blinded him to the old world as the question was posed, "Saul, Saul, why persecute thou me?" Because of that spiritual spark, Saul no longer used his Jewish name but his Roman name of Paul as he set out upon the great commission. Paul trained others, wrote letters of instructions, evangelized in several cities, and conducted five missionary journeys. It is in Paul's travels that he spread the spiritual spark in the Association's name of "Berean".

We give thanks, for it is in Paul's travels that research gives the biblical reference of "Berean," a word that appears twice in the Bible. Berean derives from the city of Brea where Paul and Silas fled to escape the Jews of Thesopolonian [Thessalonica]. The staff writer of the Forerunner's, November 2000 edition, wrote an article titled, "The Berean Example". A review of the article is an analysis of Brea and its people. The article gives the readers insight in the selection of the name by those spiritual leaders at First African Baptist Church in Darien, Georgia in 1899.

The staff writer explains why the Bereans are so special. "They were fair and noble minded, received the word with readiness, searched the scripture to see if what they were being taught was correct, observed how the messenger conducted their lives, and studied the word daily. The Bereans separated themselves from the world but still influenced the conversions of others. They embraced a love and concern for God." The writer addresses the geographical factor that is religious based and a key fact about the city. Brea has many streams of *living water* flowing through it. The writer shows parallelism of the streams of water being vital to the city and its inhabitants, just as the living water Jesus gave the woman at the well. Jesus says, "Whoever drinks of this water [from Jacob's well (verse 6)] will thirst again, but whoever drinks of the water that I shall give him will never thirst. But the water that I shall give him will become in him a fountain of water springing up into everlasting life" (verses 13-14) [John 4:].

What a powerful image of the Bereans and the Association we now serve. It is in the name that the present generation must understand to receive the word, study the word, separate from the world, but be ready to seek the conversion of others. A review of the literature identifies Sandy D. Martin's study of the African Missionary interest by the black church during the period of 1880-1915. One aspect of the black church was and remains to fulfill the great commission, go into the world and proclaim God's salvation. This legacy was set as an aspect of those spiritual men in Darien, Georgia (Black Baptist and African Mission 1880-1915).

We give thanks for Paul's travel to Athens. It is in Athens that one sees another common thread that confirms God's guidance and plan for the Association. Not only is the church of significance and the name significant, but also the city of Darien's Street is of significance. The church and the jail house are located on "Market Street" where the mobs gathered in protest. Chapters 16 and 17 of the book of Acts give reference to Paul's presence in the **market**place, where healing and teaching took place. He was locked in **jail** after casting out a demonic spirit in the **market**place, and he preached to those who were not in the Jewish synagogue. Henry Denegal [Delegal] was locked in a **jail** on Market Street. The church bell rang on Market Street. The preachers met in the church on Market Street, but above all, our Savior converted Saul to Paul, thus enhanced Paul to share the importance of "study."

The Bible speaks to God's preparation for the Leadership of the Association in the first chapter of Jeremiah verse five: "Before I formed thee in the belly I knew thee; and before thou camest forth out of the womb I sanctified thee, and I ordained thee a prophet unto the nations" (King James Version). It is God's radius of protection that has allowed those He put in place to move this Association into another century of time because He sanctified each leader with insight of growth and fortitude. We give God all glory and praise for preparation of the table as He placed eight [nine] Christian men in their mother's womb.

And so, it was not by chance that the year 1899 would begin with a rumor about the possible lynching of the Negroe [Negro] and a year of "Insurrection-Civil Disobediences". In today's society, that [kind of] "insurrection" is equivalent to "protest". No, it was not by chance that the spiritual spark would transcend time to assure the sending of a telegraph to request funding for legal support and impact the ringing of the church bell during the summer of that year. No, it was not by chance that when we looked among the persons present at the organizational meeting, there sat three of the Association's Moderators. Nor is it by chance that one Moderator is called to cross the river and form the first church for slaves on the east side of Savannah. It is not by chance that one Moderator would recognize the state of the Nation as laws were passed during his tenure. It is not by chance that after the organizational meeting of the Berean Missionary Baptist Association, the influence of the Pastors on the families in Darien, Georgia, and the ringing of the church bell, a baby was born on April 15,1900 across the river in Allendale, South Carolina. It is not by chance that one Moderator would institute a scholarship to fulfill the dream of the Association's youth to attend college and to continue their course of study into their careers' endeavors. It is not by chance that one Moderator will be called to assist in the fulfillment of a federal mandate to desegregate the schools of the southern cities; nor is it by chance that this same Moderator would confirm the definition of the word, "church," due to a fire. Lastly, it is not by chance that the Moderator for the year of our Lord, two thousand seventeen, would be the angel of a church with the motto: "come join us where the table is always spread" as he continues the legacy of partnerships with other organizations, effective communication, and the organization of the Pilgrim Baptist Church of Savannah.

It is not by chance that you, the reader, see God's guiding hand of preparation in the longevity of this Association. It was and remains the will of God, concerning each Moderator, that the Association has weathered the sands of time for one hundred seventeen years. The Association's flame could not flicker in the Savannah's Faith Based Community without the combustion kindled by continued commitment and dedication placed upon the heart of eight [nine] men with a desire to serve. God's spokespersons in years to come will possess that same heart of combustion and fortitude to serve.

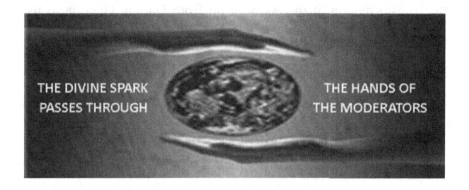

We salute each Moderator for his willingness to serve, time served, and for keeping the spiritual spark alive.

Dea. Jones writes, "the first Moderator for the Berean Missionary Baptist Association was Rev. **P.J. Butler.**" There is no listing of Rev. Butler's church, but he was from Darien, Georgia. A review of the history for First African Baptist Church of Darien, Georgia does list a Rev. Butler in its history. This writer feels safe in the conclusion that Rev. Butler laid the administrative foundation of Leadership for the Association and was guided by the spiritual spark in naming of the organization. Also, because he served during the period of the "Insurrection-Civil Disobediences" and was a resident of Darien, Georgia, this writer believes he stood among the protestors when the church bell of First African Baptist Church in Darien, Georgia rang on August 23,1899. He set the legacy of addressing social issues by forming partnerships as seen in the life of the Association and its future leaders. He played a major role in the transformation of the Association from Darien, Georgia to its permanent residence of Savannah, Georgia as the spark was passed on to the second Moderator.

Rev. W.L.P. Weston accepted the position as the second Moderator for the Berean Missionary Baptist Association and the first Moderator for the city of Savannah. Rev. Weston was pastor of Mount Zion Baptist Church. There is no record of the year his term started, but this writer calculates the first and second Moderators served a total of twenty-nine years collectively. During his tenure, we see a legacy for education of our youth. A review of the literature confirms the establishment of a school for Negroes in the city of Savannah. The Senior Researcher in Baptist History, Robert G. Gardner, notes that in 1895, the Zion Baptist Church established a school named, "Baptist High School of Savannah, Georgia". The Senior Researcher shares that in 1912 the name of the school was changed to "Berean High School or Baptist Academy, Savannah, Chatham County (African American)." Thus, we can safely say under Rev. Weston's administration, the education of our youth was a goal of the Association. The literary review of the National Baptist Convention U.S.A.'s history confirms the hosting of the National Congress during Rev. Weston's tenure in 1916.

Moderator Butler's tenure included working with a young man born March 20, 1861, in Allendale, South Carolina by the name of William S. Gray. According to the History of the American Negro, Volume II, "that young man knew at an early age of his calling to preach. He spoke of God's voice speaking to him, telling him to go to Savannah." Just as it took Jonah spending three days in the belly of the whale, so it was the same for William S. Gray to heed God's calling. He was a farmer, and for three seasons God would tell him to "go"; but it was not until the reaping of the third season's crop that he set out on his Heavenly father's business. The History books tell us that Rev. Gray compared himself to Moses as God continually told him, "Go to Savannah."

Rev. Gray, like Moses, set sights to cross the Savannah River and rendered his membership with First Bryan Missionary Baptist Church located in Yamacraw Village [in Savannah, Georgia]. But that was not God's calling upon his life, for just as Moses led the way for the children of Israel and set up the plan for Jacob to lead, so was the same for Rev. William S. Gray. It was 1885 that Rev. Gray sought consent to establish a church on the east side of Savannah for First Bryan's members. The church was built and in 1891, Father William S. Gray led a group of former slaves into what is now identified as, "The Mighty Fortress," St. John Missionary Baptist Church on the east side of Savannah, Georgia.

Not only did God direct him into pastorship of St. John, but He had him in Darien, Georgia at the organizational meeting of the Berean Missionary Baptist Association in 1899. Therefore, he had full knowledge of the spiritual spark that ignited the organization, the naming of the Association, the organizational structure of the Association, and the operations of the Association. This affirmation confirms the supernatural powers of God as He placed his chosen ones to coordinate, guide, and direct.

In 1918-1942, Rev. William S. Gray accepted the charge as the third Moderator for the Berean Missionary Baptist Association and continued to ignite the path of this Association. Two years into his leadership, the Nineteenth Amendment was ratified, August 18, 1920, giving women the Right to vote. The legacy of addressing social issues continued, for in the words of the Historian, Dea. Johnnie P. Jones, "The Women's Auxiliary to the Berean Missionary Baptist Association was organized in 1920, with an enthusiastic group of Christian women. Rev. William Gray was Moderator of the Parent Body and Pastor of St. John Baptist Church, Savannah, Georgia and deemed it necessary to organize an Auxiliary." You will read about the legacy of missionary work through the Auxiliary with service to the local community and Foreign Mission. Rev. Gray, also known as Father Gray, guided the organization for twenty-four (24) years until he passed the spark in 1943.

In 1943-1948 [Died in1944] Rev. **Eddie Daniel Davis received** the spark to serve as the fourth Moderator for the Berean Missionary Baptist Association. Rev. Davis was the pastor of First Tabernacle Missionary Baptist Church. He served as the pastor of First Tabernacle from 1910 to 1944. There are no written references for details of activities during Rev. Davis's five [one year] years of service to the Association. However, we do know that the legacy of the dream for Greenbriar Children's Center lives on in real time. As you continue to read, you will see the significance of "Partnerships" in the Association, for this writer had the opportunity to sit in the presence of Dr. Martha Wilson, a Mathematics instructor at Savannah State College (University). Dr. Wilson shared history on the requirements to organize what is now known as the graduate chapter of Alpha Kappa Alpha Sorority, Incorporated in the city of Savannah, Georgia. One requirement was to organize and complete a community service project. Dr. Wilson shared that she along with Dorothy Jamison, Quita Frankie Thompson, Mary Stephens McDew, and a fourth member needed the support of a religious organization to develop an orphanage for children. She shared that the money for the orphanage came from a rich white lady's will. There was one requirement; both organizations had to commit to annual support of the orphanage. The facts of her story are posted on the websites of Greenbriar Children's Center and Savannah College of Art and

Designs (SCAD). SCAD posted, "Greenbriar Children's Center began as the dream of five young black women who, in 1943, organized the Gamma Sigma Omega Chapter of Alpha Kappa Alpha Sorority and began to seek a community service project. The women learned that a well-known Savannah woman, Adaline [Adeline] Graham, had died and left property and funds to "whomever might start a movement to establish an orphanage for Negro children." The will stipulated, "the colored citizens of Savannah must, within a reasonable amount of time after Graham's death, make some move to establish said institution, and the colored Protestant churches of Savannah must lend their support and aid in maintaining said institution." Sorority members sought the help of black Protestant churches and the late Rev. Ralph Mark Gilbert, who was then pastor of the First African Baptist Church. Area church leaders met at First African Baptist, a move that resulted in more than 22 churches pledging support to the orphanage. A dream became reality as Greenbriar Children's Center opened on July 15, 1949. The religious organization that Dr. Wilson spoke of is the Berean Missionary Baptist Association, Inc. The organizational meeting was held at First African Baptist Church, Savannah, Georgia.

This writer can validate that both organizations are active participants with the annual donation activities that expand the monetary donations of $1,500.00 or more, toys for children, cleaning supplies, school supplies, personal toiletry items, mentorships, tutors, and the fundraiser of wrapping gifts at the mall every Christmas season, in support of the orphanage [Greenbriar Children's Center].

[Rev. S. A. Baker, 1945 – 1948 served as Moderator]

Rev. Eugene Aiken Capers, 1949-1982, received the spark for Leadership and became the fifth [sixth] Moderator for the Berean Missionary Baptist Association. Rev. Capers served as Pastor of First Evergreen Missionary Baptist Church. This young man of forty-nine years kept the five young ladies of Alpha Kappa Alpha's dream alive and set the corner stone of longevity for what was an orphanage for Negro children. The orphanage has transformed from an orphanage for Negroe [Negro] children to a center for all children. Greenbriar Children's Center has grown beyond the five young ladies' imagination. According to the Center's present website, "Greenbriar Children's Center mission is to provide services, which promote the healthy development of children and the strengthening of families. Our services include the emergency shelter, residential care, runaway/homeless programs, independent living, family preservation, early childhood development programs, and Project Safe." Rev. Capers assured thirty-three annual contributions to Greenbriar Children's Center that were pledged by churches under Rev. Davis's administration. That legacy continues as the roll call of churches, in the Association, takes place at the annual Congress of Christian Education held each summer.

Within his thirty-three years, Rev. Capers expounded upon one of the noble factors of the Berean, "study". The study of the "Word" expanded beyond the four walls of the church during his tenure. You will find the concept of the Bereans as you read through the next few pages of a scholarship, the Congress of Christian Education, the training of staff, the development of a curriculum from National certified courses, and implementation of instruction.

1983-1999 Rev. William Daniels received the spark to serve as the sixth [seventh] Moderator for the Berean Missionary Baptist Association. The native of Willacoochee, Georgia arrived to Savannah in 1931. Rev. William H. Daniels served as the pastor of Central Missionary Baptist Church of Hitch Village. He served as Moderator of the Association for seventeen years. Rev. Daniels was well known for having read the Bible seven times. Thus, this reader of the Word, guided the Association as a doer of the Word. An article, posted in the *Savannah Now* on Thursday, May 21, 1998, confirms the Association pledge, "For a Good Cause when Rev. W. H. Daniels of Berean Missionary Baptist Association of Georgia presented Greenbriar Children's Center with a check for $1,500 as part of its annual contribution. Yvette Johnson-Hagins, Executive Director of Greenbriar, accepted the check on behalf of Greenbriar."

Pastor Matthew Southall Brown, Sr., 2000-2012, in 2000, the spark passed into the hands of the seventh [eighth] Moderator for the Berean Missionary Baptist Association, Rev. Matthew Southall Brown, Sr. Can you see God's plans for the Association as the spark touches the hands of another Pastor from the Mighty Fortress, St. John Missionary Baptist Church?

During Moderator Brown's tenure, the Berean Missionary Baptist Association celebrated its centennial. The session began Wednesday, October 6, 2009 with a musical concert at First Bryan Baptist Church. The session followed on Thursday with a Bible hour and included preaching, fellowship, and Christian instruction. The objective of that session was to make plans for the next millennium. As you read on into the History, you will see how the legacy of study increased in the hands of the spark bearers for the next millennium as God prepared the Association's table. As you continue to read, can you see the Divine Spark? Can you see what Jeremiah meant [Before I formed thee in the belly I knew thee, Jeremiah 1:5] about these men's mothers and the womb, and did you find the Moderator born on April 15,1900 as you read this first part of History? Read on to view God's plan for the new millennium as History repeats itself.

Preparations for the new millennium began in the city of Savannah on July 6, 1926, with the birth of the Rev. Matthew Southall Brown. The period of preparation included Rev. Brown's ordination as a Deacon at the First African Baptist Church of Savannah. It was the very same Church where the Partnership with the Association and the young ladies of Alpha Kappa Alpha met to organize the orphanage. *The Forerunner's* article, "The Berean Example" and the *Savannah Herald's* article written by Charles Hoskins [Dr. Charles Hoskins], confirm God's selection of individuals to lead the Association. Mr. [Dr.] Hoskins writes, "Deacon Matthew S. Brown, Sr. enrolled in a three-year extension course from the American Baptist School of Theology at Nashville, Tennessee, graduating with a Bachelor of Divinity in 1961. From 1975 to 1981, he attended summer seminars and workshops at the Princeton School of Theology in Princeton, New Jersey." A key factor of the Berean is they studied the "Word". Why has this information been included in this section, you may wonder, as you read the excerpts about Rev. Matthew Southall Brown, Sr.

This writer wants you to keep notice of God's continued desire for you to study. In Nashville, Tennessee, Deans and Christian Leadership Schools are certified by the Sunday School Publishing Board.

Two years into his leadership, Rev. Brown charged the Historian, Dea. [Johnnie] Paul Jones and the History Committee with the task to develop a bound copy of the Association's history. Also, within the first two years of Rev. Brown's leadership, paperwork was filed, and on February 25, 2002, the name changed from The

Berean Missionary Baptist Association to The Berean Missionary Baptist Association, Inc, with non-profit status. Can you see God's hand upon the spark as it is passed to one who went on to deliver the opening prayer for the U.S. House of Representatives, was appointed chairperson of a twelve-member biracial school's advisory committee by Federal District Court Judge, Alexander Lawrence, and was active in the Civil Rights Movement? Just as Moderator Gray was respected, admired, and known in the community as "Father Gray," Moderator Brown was also respected, admired, and known in the community as, "Pastor to all." Both pastored the historical "Mighty Fortress," St. John Missionary Baptist Church.

Marcus Howard, a reporter for the *Savannah Now*, wrote an article titled, "Dean of Savannah Clergy Releases New Book." The title is truly appropriate for within the Congress of Christian Education's records, you will find that there were five persons certified as Deans during Pastor Brown's tenure. Please remember that all Deans are certified by the Sunday School Publishing Board in Nashville, Tennessee. In addition to the Deans' certification, there was an increase of instructors' certification. The increase in staff impacted the expansion of the curriculum, the planning for instruction, implementation of the lessons, and an increase of students to study the Word.

A review of the pages on the Congress of Christian Education and the Women Auxiliary's histories will show the legacy of partnership with the local school district for the usage of a school to host Christian Education sessions due to an increase in attendance. Also, within the review of Mr. Howard's article is a quote from Rev. Brown that explains and confirms Rev. Brown's philosophy on the need to provide an educational environment for youth. Rev. Brown stated, "Any organization be it a church, home, school, city, or town moves forward on the feet of their children. And if we don't train them well, I think you understand what will happen to that institution." It was Rev. Brown's desire to acquire a building to house the Association for future training, but he stepped down from the position in 2012. However, God had one who served as a worker from the days of his youth into his adulthood at the Association's table and who was ready to complete Rev. Brown's term.

Pastor Brown renders the torch to

Rev. Dr. Clarence "Teddy" Williams

The second millennium leader is also a native of Savannah, Georgia. He grew in study through the Berean Association as he enhanced the music of the Association. His religious education includes studies at the Billy Graham School of Evangelism (Wheaton College) and Beeson Divinity School (Samford University). "In 2004, he received the Honorary Doctorate of Christian Music Degree from the Great Commission Bible School and Seminary."

From 2013 to the present, Rev. Dr. Clarence "Teddy" Williams was elected as the eighth [ninth] Moderator of the **Berean Missionary Baptist Association, Incorporated** on October 19, 2012, at the 112th Annual Session. The historical point here is "Rev. Dr. Williams was the first to complete the term of a previous Moderator and the first

Moderator elected under the "Incorporated" title of the Association. On Saturday, January 5, 2013, the officers and member churches of the *Berean Missionary Baptist Association, Incorporated* installed its eighth [ninth] Moderator, Rev. Dr. Clarence "Teddy" Williams. God's hand is seen once again as the spark is passed to another pastor of First Tabernacle Missionary Baptist Church. He now serves as Pastor of New Pilgrim Baptist Church of Savannah.

In the first year of his service, Rev. Dr. Clarence "Teddy" Williams reviewed the organizational structure, financial operation, and the governing documents of the Association. He initiated a website, online registration, organizational chart for inclusion in the Association Manual, and Association's stationary. Included within the pages of this book, you will find the organizational chart, **the revised By-Laws,** a summation of the financial procedures, and documents from the website, http://www.thebereanassociation.org.

Rev. Williams has expanded the thrust for working with today's youth and adults by establishing partnership agreement with Shaw University, Youth Futures, Greenbriar Children's Center, American Red Cross, Savannah Regional Central Labor Council, and Queensborough Bank. He continues the legacy of "study" by bridging the gap of student enhancement. Youth Futures is an organization that focuses on At-Risk Youth while Shaw University offers a scholarship to the academically prepared youth. The Chatham Association of

Educators and the Retired Educators of Chatham Association work with the Berean Association to address legislative issues that impact the students and adults of the Savannah-Chatham County Public School System.

There were partnerships with agencies to share with the adults such concepts or topics on the work force, wages, safety, health, insurance, and financial investments. Such topics are discussed annually at the summer Congress of Christian Education and the Annual General Session. Rev. Dr. Williams utilizes technology to increase active participation, not only of the workers but also of the churches.

Rev. Williams also appointed a Conflict Resolution Committee to assist churches when they encountered issues affecting their church. He Initiated Seniors Ministry under Rev. Carolyn Dowse, completed Association By-Laws, reactivated the Laymen Ministry, appointed a Social/Civic Committee and a Strategic Planning Committee, and named Scholarships in honor of former moderators, Rev. William Daniels and Rev. Matthew Southall Brown, Sr. (Daniels/Brown Scholarship). Yes, God prepared this Moderator as he grew up enhancing the Music Ministry in the Association.

Formation of the Berean Congress of Christian Education

"History of the Congress of the Berean Association
of Georgia Christian Education"

Portions Recorded by Sis. S. Primus

In August 1969, the Association, the Sunday School, and the Baptist Training Union met at Elm Grove Baptist Church, Meridian, Georgia, Rev. J.F. Mann, Pastor. Rev. E.A. Capers, Moderator. At the close of the session, everyone was asked to think and pray for the organizing of a Congress. In 1970, at First Evergreen Baptist Church, the Congress was organized. Rev. E. A. Capers, Moderator, Rev. William Daniels, Vice Moderator, Rev. J. F. Mann, statistician were present. Dea. Spencer E. White, Sr. was elected as President and the other officers as follows:

Sis. Sadie Norris-Financial Secretary
Sis. Helen Brown, Recording Secretary
Sis Reatha Delaware, Treasurer

Dea. John Delaware, Director General
Dea. David Rankin, Dean
Sis. Ola B. Dingle, Faculty Secretary to the Dean

Instructors named:
Sis Rose Pinckney, First Bryan Missionary Baptist Church
Sis. Alfredia Shaw, First African Missionary Baptist Church
Sis. Louise Bing Roberts, First African Baptist Church
Dea. James Rickenbacker, First Tabernacle Missionary Baptist Church
Sis. Ola B. Dingle, Second Arnold Missionary Baptist Church
Sis. Ollie Pearl Grant, First Evergreen Missionary Baptist Church
Sis. Carrie Rouse, First Jerusalem Missionary Baptist Church
Sis. Emma Jean Hodge, First Tabernacle Missionary Baptist Church
Sis. Eunice Andrews, First Bryan Missionary Baptist Church

A scholarship fund was established in 1962 and named after the first President, Spencer E. White. The first recipient was Sis. Betty West, who later became Dean and General Dean of the Congress. Dea. Spencer E. White did a wonderful job through Christ and the support of the workers. Prior to the Congress being formed, the Sunday School and BTU Convention of the Berean Association was in operation. During the Second year of the Congress in 1971, there were 16 instructors and 101 students.

A discussion arose on selecting a Vice President. Dea. White asked members to elect someone for the position, and Dea. Robert L Everson, of Elm Grove, was elected. Dea. White died in 1984, so Dea.

Everson became President of the Congress in 1984, and Dea. Willie Waddell of St John Baptist was elected Vice President. Sis. Ola B. Dingle was elected Congress Dean and with input, Sis. Betty West was added as the Assistant Dean. Sis. Betty West was elected Dean upon Sis. Dingle's death. Sis. Betty West has served the Congress since its conception in 1971.

The Congress continued growing under Dea. Everson's and Dea. Waddell's leadership. God strengthened and kept them. Dea. David Rankin resigned in 1995, after eleven years of service as the Dean.

Dea. Waddell resigned in May of 1990 due to illness, and Sis. Janie Bowers was elected Vice President. Other positions listed follow:

- ➢ Deacon Ernest Coleman, Director General and Associate Dean
- ➢ Bro. Paul Gibbs Assistant Director General
- ➢ Sis. Mildred Brownlee Johnson, First African Baptist Missionary Church, Secretary to the Faculty (relieving Sis. Dingle to become Dean); Sis. Brownlee resigned as Faculty Secretary in 1979 at Elm Grove Baptist Church of Meridian
- ➢ Sis. Suzanna J. Primus served for sixteen (16) years along with Sis. Viola Baker and Sis. Alvena Baker. In 1972, the First Secretarial Class was organized. Sis. Birdie Gordon of First Bryan Missionary Baptist Church was the instructor. It was a four-year course at a cost of two dollars per year. In 1976, the first graduates received

certificates. They were Sis. Sadie Evans, Sis Suzanna J. Primus, of Central Baptist Church in Hitch Village, Sis. Ola Osborne, Zion Hill Baptist, Sis. Jordan of Elm Grove, Meridian Ga; Sis. Theresa Porter of St. John. Two of the five are deceased at the time of Sis. Primus's records.

Dea. Ernest Coleman served well until his death. Sis. Helen Jones of St. John was selected as the Director General. Sis. Lillian Spencer was Corresponding Secretary. The appointed Committee members were Dea. David Rankins, Sis Sadie Norris, Sis. Thomasina White, and Dea. Robert Everson. Assistant Deans were Sis. Yvonne Warren 1988 and Sis. Marion Marshall. Sis. Primus writes, "since our last session, we have had many members ill, at home, or in the hospital. We are happy to say they have improved and still carry on. I and others were in sorrow to hear of the death of Deacon Rankin this year. It was a shock and a great loss; the work he did spoke for him. A copy will be given to the secretary of this organization. Prayfully submitted." Dea. Robert Everson of Meridian, GA became President of the Congress of Christian Education. After Dea. Everson resigned, Rev. Timothy Sheppard, Pastor of Central Missionary Baptist Church of Thunderbolt, was elected President, and Rev. Matthew Southall Brown, Jr. of Union Baptist [First Union Baptist] was elected Vice President at the 112th Annual Session held at First Nazareth Missionary Baptist Church where Rev. Guy Hodges III was the Pastor.

Scholarship to Leadership

In 1963, plans got under way to raise money to award at least one scholarship. The scholarship was named for the Congress of Christian Education's first President, Dea. Spencer E. White. The first recipient of the one hundred dollars scholarship was Miss Betty Simmons, now known as Dean Betty West.

Dean West had a vision to establish a school to serve the spiritual needs of the Savannah and surrounding communities. The only way students could receive credit, the school needed a certified instructional staff. To have a certified instructional staff, she needed Deans. Thus, Dean Betty West was guided by the Spiritual spark on the Damascus Road as she set out to increase the number of Deans and certified instructors from 1987 to 2014. Dean West stepped aside due to her husband's illness, but she still stands in mentor mode for the Association.

Three persons were certified to become Deans through the Berean Congress of Christian Education during Rev. Daniel's tenure. They were mentored by Dean Betty West and certified with the Sunday School Publishing Board in Nashville, Tennessee: Sis. Janie B. Bowers in 1987, Dea. Robert West, 1999, and Sis. Gwen Davis of Zion Association. Five persons were certified as Deans during Rev. Matthew Southall Brown, Sr.'s tenure.

Dean Betty West mentored and presented the mentees as Acting Deans of the Berean Congress under Director/Dean West, and the sessions of the Congress were under the new ruling curriculum of the Sunday School Publishing Board Nashville, Tennessee. The new ruling included Mentor Dean, Dean's Internship, Acting Dean of a certified Congress of Christian Education, and Dean of a Session or Certified Leadership School. Acting Deans for Certification in the Berean Congress are as follows:

38th Session 2007 Sis. Cynthia Fearbry

40th Session 2009 Dr. Deloise C. Thorne

41st Session 2010 Dr. Mary A. Brown

42nd Session 2011 Dr. Anna Marie James

43rd Session 2012 Sis. Kathy Morgan

The face of Congress changed from a three-day session to a four-day session. The offering of electives to prepare for the Youth Rally meant an increase of seat time. The enrollment has not only increased among the youth but the young adults, adults, and seasoned saints. Such an increase is why Pastor Brown sought to purchase a building for classroom space. The Association has depended upon the local school facilities to house its students. The increase of enrollment has resulted in departments with a Dean Supervisor of instruction. The Dean's task is to assist with design of the curriculum, to assure ample course offerings, to seek instructors to serve in the classroom setting, to review the course syllabus for the course offerings, and above all, to obtain certified staff for Certificate of Progress Program (COPP) courses. The Congress's process has transitioned from on-site to pre-registration via e-mail, slow mail, or under the present Moderator Williams's "on-line", through credit card payments.

EXCERPTS OF DEAN WEST'S LETTER OF REQUEST FOR LEADERSHIP SCHOOL
MAY 23, 1985

Malone Sr, Director of Christian

En closed is the necessary material to request 1985 accreditation for the "Berean Missionary Congress of Christian Educat Standard Leadership School) to be held Augu 6-9, 1985 at First Tabernacle Baptist Church. Rev. W. N Robinson pastor; 310 Alic Street, Savannah, Georgia.

1. All teacher are Certified untill 1986.
2. ~~The~~ Dean Mrs. O. B. Dingle died March 24, Betty Jean West is a Certifie will head the school.
         We are in need of following forms;
                    Thank

Everything was draft of letter to be typed and mailed.....

SPARK OF DIVINE INTERVENTION

THE SPARK
WOMEN'S SUFFRAGE

The spark transcends over the period of time as the Association moves forward and Rev. William Gray serves as the Moderator. It is during Rev. Gray's tenure that the country is impacted by Women's Rights, the passing of the Nineteenth Amendment, and the Association's organization for a women's auxiliary.

"The Women's Auxiliary to the Berean Missionary Baptist Association was organized in 1920 with an enthusiastic group of Christian women. The Rev. William Gray, Moderator of the Parent body and Pastor of St. John Missionary Baptist Church, deemed it necessary to organize a Women's Auxiliary. Prayers were offered, wheels were put into motion, churches were notified and responded by sending elected women from their missionary societies to Waycross, Georgia for the organizational meeting where Rev. Starling was Pastor.

The first officers were the following: President, Mrs. M.M. Mills, First Bryan Baptist Church Savannah; First Vice President, Mrs. Chattie Sims, St. John Baptist Church, Savannah; 2nd Vice President, Mrs. J. S. Moody, First Tabernacle Baptist Church, Savannah; 3rd Vice President, Mrs. Mary Major, White Oak Baptist Church, Montieth; Secretary, Mrs. Emma D. Perry, First Bryan Baptist Church; Corresponding Secretary, Mrs. M.S. Grant, Darien, Georgia; Treasurer, Mrs. Ellen Brown, Bethlehem Baptist Church, Savannah, Georgia.

The Auxiliary officers in 1923 were the following: President, Sis, Inez L. Davis; Vice President, Sis Marie Green; 2nd Vice President, Sis. Ellen Roberson; 3rd Vice President, Sis Lillian Brown; Secretary, Sis. Annie Rickenbacker; Treasurer, Sis. Lizzie Cox; Chairman of Board, Sis. Rosa B. Viss; Auditors, Sis. E. J. Williams and Sis. Etta Brown; Historian, Sis. L.L. Allen; Junior Director, Sis. B.E. Foster; Assistant Junior Directors, Sis. Rosa Johnson and Sis. M.A. Scarboro; Field Worker, Sis. Rosa Lovett.

The Women's Auxiliary continued working together in Jesus's name, and in 1955 the officers were the following: President, Sis. Marie D. Green; 1st Vice President Sis T. Jones; 2nd Vice President, Sis. G.

Dingle; Treasurer, Sis Allie Gordan; Recording Secretary, Sis. A.L. Graves; Financial Secretary, Sis. M.G. Johnson; Chairman of Board, Sis. Rosa B. Voss; Auditors, Sis. Maggie Canty; Music Director, Sis. E.H. Perry, and Assistant Music Director, Sis. Lillian Wilson [See Appendix B, The Journey of the Berean Baptist Association Women's Auxiliary, 1920 – 1982 for an in-depth chronicle of the Women's Auxiliary].

> The Adjourned Sesson of the Berean Missionary Baptist Association of Georgia met with the Bolton Street Baptist Church, 821West Board Street on January 30,1974, Rev. Thomas Pryor, Pastor, Rev. E. Aikens Capers, Moderator, Sis. Sarah White Auxiliary President.

> The Seventy-Six Session was held with First Bryan Baptist Church, 575 West Bryan Street on October 8-10, 1975, Rev. Arthur D. Sims, Pastor, Rev. Eugene A. Capers, Moderator and Sis. Sarah White, Auxiliary President.

> The Adjourned Sesson was held with First Friendship Baptist Church, 836 Wheaton Street on January 28, 1976, Rev. Henry Boles, Pastor, Rev. Eugene A. Capers, Moderator, Sis. Sarah White, Auxiliary President.

> The Seventy-Seventh Session is not recorded, but the Adjourned Sesson was held with the Macedonia Baptist Church, 508 East Jones Street on January 26,1977, Rev. Levi Moore, Minister, Rev. Eugene A. Capers, Moderator, Sis. Sarah White, Auxiliary President.

> The Seventy-Eighth Session was held with St. John Baptist Church, 526 Hartridge Street on October 5-7, 1977, Rev. Matthew S. Brown, Pastor, Rev. Eugene A. Capers, Moderator, and Sis. Sarah White, Auxiliary President.

➢ The Adjourned Sesson was held with the Tremont Temple Missionary Baptist Church, 1110 West Board Street on January 25,1978, Rev. George J. Faison, Pastor, Rev. Rev. Eugene A. Capers, Moderator, Sis. Sarah White, Auxiliary President.

➢ The Seventy-Ninth Session was held with Central Baptist Church, Hitch Village on October 4-6, 1978, Rev. Williams Daniel, Pastor, Rev., Daniels, Moderator, and Sis. Sarah White, Auxiliary President.

There is no record of the Annual Session for 1978

➢ The Eightieth Annual Session was held with First Tabernacle Baptist Church on October 10-12, 1979, Rev. W.N. Robinson, Pastor. A session was held at Central Baptist Church, Hitch Village on October 4-6, 1978, Rev. Eugene A. Capers, Moderator, and Sis. Sarah White, Auxiliary President.

➢ The Adjourned Sesson was held with Macedonia Baptist Church, 508 East Jones Street, Rev. Archie Fields, Pastor, January 30, 1980, Rev. Eugene A. Capers, Moderator, Sis. Sarah White, Auxiliary President.

➢ The Eighty-first Session was held with the Mt. Zion Missionary Baptist Church, 1008 West Board Street (MLK), Rev. Robert Twyman, Pastor, October 8-10, 1980, Rev. Eugene A. Capers, Moderator, and Sis. Sarah White, Auxiliary President.

➢ The Adjourned Sesson was held with Bethlehem Baptist Church, 1008 May Street, on January 26, 1983, Rev. William Daniels, Moderator, Sis. Sarah White, Auxiliary President.

Sis. Sarah White became ill and moved to New York City. Sis. Annie Lizzie Ross became the Women's Auxiliary President. When Sis. Ross became ill after serving for six years and went to be with the Lord, Sis. Florrie Scriven became President in 1992. This writer can acknowledge that Sis Florrie Scriven served as President of the Women's Auxiliary during this period. It is a period wherein the Auxiliary focused on Foreign Mission and children. Every year the Auxiliary hosted a week of activities for the children of the Savannah-Chatham County Public School System during Spring Break. They continued the art of Bible Study and elective classes, and they visited nursing homes in Savannah, GA and Pooler, GA during Spring Break. The program is parallel to the hours of a regular school day. This administration provided lunch in parks and held an Annual Day of Youth Prayer at parks in Savannah.

Foreign Mission was also an important focus of this administration. Diane Severance writes in Church History how a man name Lott Corey became a preacher, bought his freedom, and reached back to Africa. He is considered the first Baptist slave to reach back, take the Word to Africa, and develop colonies there to reduce slavery by helping the people there to live better. According to the *Savannah Tribune*, "In 1999, Sis. Scriven saw the need to plan and coordinate a city-wide drive, collecting monetary contributions, baby items, clothing, food, etc. to aid the people living in the mountainous, remote area of Tapio, Haiti. She has since fervently continued her work to support the Haitian country by accompanying health practitioners and others on five tours to Foreign Mission Tapio to give medical assistance and to spread God's Word and love." She humbly resigned from the position at the 114th Annual Session.

SPARK OF DIVINE INTERVENTION
WITH REVISIONS

Technology has truly enhanced The Berean Missionary Baptist Association, Inc.'s distribution of information to each Church, its Pastor, and its members. The following information gives you insight of the Association's growth in the second millennium.

ORGANIZATIONAL CHART FOR THE STRUCTURE OF THE ASSOCIATION

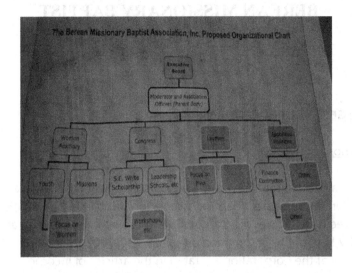

FINANCIAL STRUCTURE OF THE ASSOCIATION

Every department of the organizational structure had its Treasurer, Financial Secretary, and separate Bank Accounts. That meant funds were deposited and dispensed from several accounts within the Association. That [process] is no longer the case; the financial procedure changed under Moderator Williams. All funds were consolidated into one account with one Treasurer and one Financial Secretary for the Association. The Treasurer now collects all funds, and it is recorded by the Financial Secretary. Funds are dispersed based on a voucher with a written receipt attached. Thus, each auxiliary or session has a line-item budget with all funds being deposited or dispersed through the General Account.

BEREAN MISSIONARY BAPTIST ASSOCIATION, INC. BY-LAWS

Title 1: GENERAL PROCEDURES

1.1 Purpose of By-Laws

These bylaws constitute the code of rules for the regulation and management of the Berean Missionary Baptist Association, *Inc.,* (the "Corporation") as authorized by its articles of incorporation. These by-laws were duly adopted as the by-laws of the Corporation on January 30, 2002, in order to fulfill the objectives of the Corporation as stated in the articles of incorporation and The Georgia Nonprofit Corporation Code, (the "Code"), and to exercise the powers conferred upon the Corporation under the Code section 302.

1.2 Registered Office and Agent

The holder of the office of Moderator of the Corporation shall serve as the registered agent of the Corporation for the duration of his or her tenure. The registered address of the Corporation shall be that of the Moderator. The address and name of the Moderator shall be filed annually with the Georgia Secretary of State's Office as required by the Code.

1.3 Authorized Business Office

Either the board of directors or the membership of the Corporation may establish one or more offices for the conduct of business within this state, whenever, circumstances shall warrant.

1.4 Procedural Rules at Meetings

It is understood that in the transaction of its business, the meetings of the Corporation, its board of directors and its divisions may be conducted with

Proposed Revision October 2013

informality; however, this informality does not apply to procedural requirements in the articles of incorporation, these bylaws, or the Code. When circumstances warrant, any meeting or a portion of a meeting may be conducted according to generally understood principles of parliamentary procedures or a recognized procedural authority. The procedural reference authority for the Corporation is designated as the latest edition of Robert's Rules of order, Newly Revised.

Title 2 MEMBERSHIPS

2.1 Eligibility for membership

Membership in the Corporation is open to individuals and Baptist churches who believe that Jesus Christ is the Son of God who gave His life for our sins and who is now seated at the right hand of God interceding for the Saints. All churches who become members of the Corporation must designate an official representative who shall receive all notices. Each church shall have five votes for voting purposes at all membership meetings.

2.2 Procedure for Membership

Membership in the corporation may be attained by invitation of the Corporation to a Baptist church and/or by request of any organized Baptist church. At any meeting of membership or the board of directors, the names of prospective members shall be presented to the Moderator of the Corporation. The Moderator shall present such prospective members to the membership for approval at the next meeting of the membership of the Corporation. After approval, the prospective member must register with the Secretary of the Board of Directors. Membership status will be conferred upon the prospective member once registration is complete.

2.3 Benefits of Membership/Voting Rights/Powers

Each member church shall have four votes. Members elect the officers of the divisions of the Corporation as designated in Sections 3.2. Such election takes place at the first regular meeting of the membership during the second week of October. Unless otherwise provided in the articles incorporation, these bylaws, or the Code, the affirmative vote of a majority of those members casting a vote on a matter, in the presence of a quorum, is necessary to adopt a motion. Unless otherwise provided in the articles of incorporation or these bylaws, the affirmative vote of a plurality of members casting a vote in an election, in the presence of a quorum, is necessary to the election of a nominee for any position in the Corporation.

2.4 Meetings of Members

(1) Location of Meetings

Any meeting of the membership of the Corporation may be held at any place in the United States. Although the designation of a usual meeting date, time, or location is reserved to membership of the Corporation, the board of directors or the membership may determine a different location for a particular meeting as circumstances warrant.

(2) Meeting Times

The membership of the Corporation shall meet at least three times per year. The first meeting shall take place during the last week of January, the second meeting shall take place during the last week of July, and the third meeting of the Corporation shall take place during the second week of October. The third meeting of the Corporation shall be, in addition to any other business which may be before the Corporation, to electing officers for the divisions of the Corporation and as such the third meeting shall be considered the annual meeting of the Corporation.

(3) Special Meetings How Called

Special meetings of the Corporation may be called for any purpose whatsoever, at any other time by: (1) the Chairman of the board of directors, (2) the Vice Chairman of the board of directors, and any three members of the board of directors, or a written demand of five percent (5%) of the **Corporation** in good standing, filed with the Secretary of the board of directors. The purpose

Proposed Revision October 2013

of the meeting must be stated in the notice. The notice of the special meeting is to be sent to all members in good standing.

(4) Quorum

The presence of twenty percent (20%) of the members in good standing and entitled of vote constitutes a quorum for the transaction of business at meetings of the Corporation. Once a quorum is established at any meeting of the Corporation, it is presumed to exist for the balance of that meeting.

(5) Proxies

The Corporation shall not make use of nor honor any proxies. No member may use proxies to vote on any matter before the Corporation.

(6) Records Inspections

Members shall have the right to review the records of the Corporation as maintained by the Secretary of the board of directors and by the various secretaries of the divisions of the Corporation. The board of directors or the membership may adopt any needful rules or regulations reasonably necessary to facilitate such right to inspect.

2.5 Notice of Meetings

The Secretary of the board of directors, with the assistance of the recording secretaries of the divisions of the Corporation, will give notice of the time, date, and location of each meeting of the membership of the Corporation not less than fifteen (15) days or greater than thirty (30) days before the scheduled meeting date. Normally, the notice is to be sent by mail to the address of each member in good standing as reflected in the Corporation's membership roster. If the member is a church, then the notice shall be sent to the designated representative of that member. Any notice mailed first class shall be effective upon dispatch, or when received, if transmitted by any other means. In emergencies where fifteen (15) days cannot be given, notice may be made by a reasonable means if made to all members in good

Page 4 of 15

standing as directed by the board of directors. All notices must include the purpose or agenda for the meeting to which the notice pertains.

2.6 Membership Dues and Registration

A member must be in good standing in order to be eligible to receive notice of a meeting and be entitled to vote at a meeting of the membership. A member is in good standing on the rosters when all membership dues have been paid and the member has provided the Secretary of the board of directors with a current address and phone number for the membership roster. In the case of a church membership, the church must provide the Secretary with the name and address of their designated representative. For purposes of eligibility to vote, a member must be in good standing at the time the secretary of the board of directors sends the notice of the meeting.

2.7 Resignation from Membership

Any member wishing to resign his, her or its membership in the Corporation may do so in writing and such writing shall state the date of effectiveness of such resignation. In the case of a church, the resignation letter shall only be effective if sent by that church's designated representative. The letter should be sent to the Secretary of the board of directors. Within ten (10) days of receipt of any letter of resignation, the Secretary will notify the Moderator. There shall be no rebate or refund or rescission of dues or fees. Any member who resigns his membership remains obligated to the Corporation for any changes, assessments, dues, fees or amount that is outstanding as of the effective date the member resigned.

Title 3. CORPORATION DIVISIONS

3.1 Number and Name

There shall be four divisions of the Corporation: The Executive Division, The Women's Division, The Laymen's Division and the Congress of Christian Education.

Proposed Revision October 2013

The daily operations and activities of each division shall be conducted by the officers of each division as elected by the membership during the annual meeting of members in October.

3.2 Division Officers

(1) The officers of the Executive Division shall be as follows:

- Moderator

- 1st Vice-Moderator

- 2nd Vice-Moderator

- Clerk

- Treasurer

- Secretary

(2) The officers of the Women's Divisions shall be as follows:

- President

- 1st Vice President

- 2nd Vice President

- Secretary

(3) The officers of the Congress of Christian Education shall be as follows:

- President

- Vice President

- Secretary

Page 6 of 15

- Dean of the Congress

- Director General

(4) The officers of the Laymen's Division shall be as follows:

- President

- Vice President

- Secretary

3.3 Duties

The officers of each of the divisions may exercise all powers granted to them as they determine to be expedient and necessary for the interests of their particular division of the Corporation subject to the articles of incorporation, these bylaws or the Code, and to the review, direction and approval of the board of directors, and the review and direction of the membership of the Corporation.

3.4 Division Meetings

Each division of the Corporation shall meet as many or as few times as the officers of such division shall deem necessary and proper, provided however that there shall be at least one meeting of each division annually.

3.5 Election Process

The election of officers for the divisions of the Corporation will be conducted in accordance with the procedures outlined in this section or elsewhere in these bylaws and shall be as follows:

> (1) A nomination committee, appointed by the Moderator, will compile nominations for each position in each division. The Nomination Committee may make nominations in its own right.

Proposed Revision October 2013

A nomination may be made by any member in good standing, including self-nominations, or by the Nomination Committee. No nominations will be placed on the annual election ballot unless: (a) the nominee is an active member in good standing, (b) the nominee is eighteen years of age or older, and (c) the nominee has affirmatively consented to the nomination.

(2) The final list of nominees will be submitted to the Secretary of the board of directors no later than 60 days after the Adjourned Session.

(3) The election shall be conducted by secret ballot on the third day of the annual session at the annual meeting of the membership. The board of directors is authorized to adopt any procedures or rules reasonably necessary to insure the integrity of the election.

3.6 Tenure

(1) Elected officers of the corporation shall be elected for a four year term, and shall not be eligible to serve more than two consecutive terms in the same office. After being out of office for one term, a person may seek and be eligible for re-election to that office. This provision regarding tenure and term limits shall apply to all board of directors. However, this provision shall not preclude term-limited officers from being elected to different offices.

(2) In the event of vacancies in office that occur prior to the end of a term, any person elected or confirmed to a vacated office shall serve the unexpired term of the person whose office was vacated. Service in an unexpired term shall not prohibit eligibility to election or confirmation to two consecutive terms in that office.

Title 4. BOARD OF DIRECTORS

<u>4.1 Number and Composition</u>

The Board of Directors shall number 19. Each member of the Corporation elected as an officer of a division of the Corporation as listed in Section 3.2, shall automatically hold a seat on the Board of Directors. The Board of Directors shall also appoint a director at large from the membership.

<u>4.2 Terms of Service</u>

Directors shall serve as long as they hold an office in a division of the Corporation. When a Director ceases to be an officer in a division of the Corporation, he or she shall also cease to serve as Director.

<u>4.3 Powers</u>

(1) The Moderator of the Executive Division of the Corporation shall automatically be designated and hold the office of the Chairman of the Board of the Corporation. The 1st Vice Moderator of the Executive Division shall automatically be designated and hold the office of Vice-Chairman of the Board of Directors; the Treasurer of the Executive Division of the Corporation shall automatically be designated and hold the office of Treasurer of the Board of Directors; and the Clerk of the Executive Division shall automatically be designated and hold the office of secretary of the Board of Directors.

(2) The board of directors may exercise all powers granted to it as they determine to be expedient and necessary for the interests of the Corporation subject to the articles of incorporation, these bylaws, or the Code, and the review and direction of the membership of the Corporation.

Proposed Revision October 2013

(3) If some catastrophic event occurs that precludes the Corporation or the board of directors from assembling, then those directors who are capable of assembling, either in person or through a communications system, permitted all of the participants hear each other, shall convene as required and take any necessary action to preserve the Corporation until the emergency ceases. Quorum shall consist of one-half of the directors who participate in the initial emergency session. Each emergency session shall be convened by any manner of notice reasonable, prudent, or practicable in the circumstances. The available director shall designate as many members of the Corporation as necessary to serve as acting directors so that there are 19 persons serving as acting directors for the Corporation until the emergency conditions cease. The acting board of directors may exercise any and all emergency powers authorized under the Code, in the name of the Corporation, without regard to requirements of membership approval, if the action taken is reasonably necessary during the presence of emergency conditions.

4.4 Meetings

The board of directors will hold at least three regular meetings during each calendar year, during the calendar month before the month of the normally scheduled date of the regular and annual meetings of the Corporation under section 2.4 (2), and may call any other regular meetings of the board of directors, or special meetings of the board of directors, at the call of (a) the Chairman, (b) the vice-chairman, or (c) any two directors.

Following their election, but prior to the date upon which they will take office, the newly elected board of directors will meet in joint session with the outgoing board of directors for an organizational session, at which they will review all pending matters before the outgoing board, permit the new to organize its affairs, and establish a fixed meeting schedule as to the regular board meeting held prior to the scheduled regular meetings of the membership of the Corporation. Any matter relating to the affairs of the Corporation may be brought before the board unless notice of the matter is required to be included in the notice of the board of directors meeting. Notice of each special meeting is to be sent to each director by United States mail, postage prepaid, addressed to the address of record in the membership roster, at least two (2) days prior to the special meeting. Where circumstances require a meeting on less than two (2) days written and mailed notice, such notification of each member of the board of directors may also be made by any other reasonable method. At board of director's meetings, quorums consist of four (4) members; no proxy votes may be used.

4.5 Use of Communication Devices for Board Meetings

The board of directors or any Corporation committee may use a contemporaneous communications system in which all participants in the meeting can hear each other.

Participation in a meeting by this system constitutes the presence of the participant at this meeting.

4.6 Voting: Quorum

Each Director has one vote on the board of directors. A quorum exists when at least eleven (11) directors are present. Once quorum is established, all matters put to a vote before the board of directors will require the affirmative vote of many of the directors voting on the matter, in the presence of a quorum, unless a greater majority is required by these bylaws, the articles of the incorporation or the Code. The participation of a majority of the directors, whether present in person or through a contemporaneous communications system constitute a quorum of the board in order to conduct business. In the event that fewer than a majority, but at least one third of the directors are participating, then the board of directors is authorized to consider and make recommendations on any matter, action upon which is viewed as appropriate in the circumstances for action by the membership either at a meeting, by written consent, or to call a special meeting of the membership as provided in section 2.4(3)

Proposed Revision October 2013

4.7 Vacancies

When a vacancy occurs or will occur on the board of directors, then that vacancy is filled by the vote of the membership at the next regular or special meeting of the membership.

4.8 Written Consent Action by Board

Any action required by law or permitted to be taken at any meeting of the board of directors may be taken without a meeting, if a written consent setting forth the action so taken is signed by many of the directors. This consent is equivalent to a vote of the board of directors during a meeting with a quorum and is to be filed and recorded with the minutes of the corporation's board of directors. The directors who did not sign the consent action shall be given notice of the action as soon as practicable, but no later than the next membership meeting after the written consent action is signed by sufficient number of directors.

4.9 Duties of Corporation Officers

Each director of the Corporation, who is elected to the Board of Directors as an officer of the Corporation, exercises the following responsibility pertaining to their office, in addition to any other duty imposed on that office by the articles of incorporation, these bylaws, the Code, or by vote of the membership or the board of directors of the Corporation. Duties follow:

(1) The chairman presides at all meetings of the board of directors and the membership of the Corporation; reports on the activities of the Corporation to the membership at each meeting of the corporation; oversees the activities of the Corporation, and reports on those matters determined appropriate to the board of directors and the membership of the Corporation.

(2) The Vice-Chairman presides at all meetings of the board of directors or the membership of the Corporation in the absence of the Chairman, and in the case of a vacancy in the office of the Chairman, act as Chairman until a new chairman is elected by the membership under section 4.7 of these bylaws.

In addition, the Vice-Chairman oversees the operation of the Corporation committees and reports on those matters determined to be appropriate to the board of directors and the membership of the Corporation.

(3) The secretary shall maintain and provide access to the records of the Corporation as required by the Code; records the minutes of all proceedings of the board of directors and of the membership of the Corporation; maintains a current roster of the membership of the Corporation; maintains the eligible membership list for each record date as required by the Code and these bylaws, and reports on these matters to the board of directors and the membership of the Corporation.

(4) The Treasurer maintains the financial records of the Corporation; prepares the annual accounting and financial statements of the Corporation for the annual meeting of the membership of the Corporation (which may be prepared by a certified public accountant when authorized by the board of directors); and reports on these matters to the board of directors and the membership of the Corporation. The Treasurer will assist the Secretary in the counting of ballots in any election of the Corporation.

4.10 Financial Regulations

This section outlines certain policies and practices as to the financial procedures of the Corporation

(1) Any expenditure, totaling five hundred dollars ($500.00) or more of corporate funds, may not be made unless approved by the membership of the Corporation, or unless the expenditure is part of an ongoing project approved by the membership of the Corporation.

(2) No other expenditure may be made unless approved by the board of directors or the membership.

(3) Expenditures from a special account, based upon revenues into that account for a designated project or activity are subject to review only by the

Proposed Revision October 2013

supervising committee, but the status of that account will be regularly reported to the board of directors and the membership.

(4) The signatory on any bank account and the depository institution for that account is established by the board of directors through an appropriate resolution.

(5) Any director, committee chairman, committee member, or any member of the Corporation may be reimbursed for their actual and necessary expenses when reasonably incurred on behalf of the Corporation. No director, committee chairman, committee member, or member of the Corporation may receive any salary, fees, compensation, commission or other payment for rendering specific services to the Corporation.

(6) The Corporation's fiscal year runs from the first day of October to the last day of September.

4.11 Board Committees and Appointed Positions

(1) The board of directors may establish such committees, composed of at least three members of the board of directors as it determines to be necessary and proper from time to time. The membership of such committees shall be composed solely of directors; but if the committee's charge and function does not involve the management responsibility for the affairs of the Corporation, then persons who are not currently directors, but who have served as directors within the past two years may also be designated to serve on a board committee. Board committees may not exercise the authority of the board of directors when prohibited by the Code.

(2) The moderator and board of directors may appoint needed committees and positions to ensure a smooth operation of the corporation. These positions must be justifiable.

4. 12 Limitation of Service

No person may simultaneously hold more than two major positions in the Corporation. To this limitation, a "major position" only includes the offices of Chairman, vice-Chairman, Secretary of Treasurer.

Title 5. INDEMNIFICATION, REMOVAL AND AMENDMENTS

5.1 Indemnification

No amendments to the by-laws of the Corporation shall be made unless adopted by two-thirds of the voting members affirmatively voting, with a quorum present at a meeting the notice for which specifically stated that an amendment to the by-laws of the Corporation was a purpose of the meeting and would be voted on at such meeting. Once adopted, any change to these bylaws is immediately effective, unless some later date is designated in the amendment proposal.

A LIST OF FIFTY-ONE CHURCHES IN
THE BEREAN ASSOCIATION

Abyssinia Missionary Baptist
Church
Bethel Baptist Church
Bethlehem Baptist Church
Bolton Street Baptist Church
Brampton Baptist Church
Brownsville Baptist Church
Bunn Memorial Baptist Church
Central Baptist Church (Old Fort)
Central Missionary Baptist Church
(Thunderbolt, GA)
Christ Memorial Baptist Church
Clifton Baptist Church
College Park Baptist Church
Connors Temple Baptist Church
First African Missionary Baptist
Church (East Savannah)
First Ebenezer Baptist Church
First Evergreen Missionary
Baptist Church
First Friendship Baptist Church
First Metropolitan Baptist Church
First Mt. Bethel Baptist Church
First Mt. Calvary Baptist Church
First Nazareth Missionary Baptist
Church
First Smyrna Baptist Church
First Tabernacle Missionary
Baptist Church
First Union Missionary Baptist
Church
Greater Friendship Baptist Church
Happy Home Baptist Church

Historic First African Baptist
Church
Historic First Bryan Baptist
Church
Historic Second African Baptist
Church
Jonesville Baptist Church of
the P.A.W.
Litway Baptist Church
Macedonia Baptist Church
Mt. Herman Baptist Church
Mt. Moriah Baptist Church
Mt. Olivet Baptist Church
Mt. Tabor Baptist Church
Mt. Zion Baptist Church
New Generation Full Gospel Baptist
New Zion Baptist Church
Pilgrim Baptist Church of
Savannah
Richfield Baptist Church
Second Arnold Missionary Baptist
Church
Second Ebenezer Baptist Church
Second St. John Missionary Baptist
Church
St. John Divine Baptist Church
St. John Missionary Baptist
Church
Thankful Baptist Church
Tremont Temple Missionary
Baptist Church
Trinity Baptist Church
True Love Baptist Church
Zion Hill Baptist Church

HISTORICAL FIRST AFRICAN BAPTIST CHURCH

The present and 17th Pastor,
Rev. Thurmond N. Tillman

"First African Baptist Church was organized in 1773 under the leadership of Reverend George Leile. In May of 1775, he was ordained as the pastor, and December of 1777 the church was officially constituted as a body of organized believers. Under the leadership of the 3rd Pastor, Reverend Andrew C. Marshall, the congregation obtained the property where the present sanctuary stands. Marshall also organized the first black Sunday school in North America and changed the name of the church from "First Colored Baptist" to "First African Baptist". The sanctuary was completed in 1859 under the direction of the 4th Pastor, Reverend William J. Campbell.

The sanctuary still contains many of the historical elements that have allowed the congregation to preserve much of its rich history. The stained-glass windows installed during the Pastorate of Reverend George Gibbons, 5th Pastor, can still be found along the edifice. A stained-glass window of Rev. George Leile is located outside, in front of the church.

First African Baptist Church has been a place of leadership and service since its inception. Reverend Emmanuel King Love, 6th Pastor, led the movement to establish Savannah State University, formerly known as Georgia State Industrial College for Colored Youth. Rev. Love also played a big role in the establishment of Morehouse College in Atlanta, GA; Paine College in Augusta, GA.

The church served as the largest gathering place for blacks and whites to meet during the time of segregation. In Savannah, GA, some blacks were not allowed to march with their graduating class. Instead, they had separate ceremonies which were held at First African Baptist Church.

The civil rights museum in Savannah, GA is named in honor of former pastor, Rev. Dr. Ralph Mark Gilbert, "for his courageous work during the Civil Rights movement in the South." Reverend Thurmond N. Tillman currently serves as the 17th pastor of the church. He was called to serve as pastor in 1982. He serves on many organization boards that help empower the people of Savannah, GA. Our present mission is to "Seek God, Shape Lives, and Serve the World."

FIRST JERUSALEM MISSIONARY BAPTIST CHURCH

First Jerusalem Missionary Baptist Church was founded on November 29, 1881. The church began meeting in the home of Deacon Samuel and Sister Etta Williams on 41st and Anderson Street. The couple eventually bought property at 219 West 45th Street and erected a temple where they would work to gain souls for the Kingdom of God. Claiborne Curtis was ordained and elected as the first pastor of First Jerusalem Missionary Baptist Church. Many years later, in 1909, a storm wrecked the church and worship service was held in a small building in the rear. The church was rebuilt in 1916 but was destroyed by fire in 1938. A new church was built in 1947 and was dedicated in September 1950. In 1978, the church purchased property on West 52nd Street with plans of building a new house of worship.

In 1981, the 100th Church Anniversary was celebrated, and the theme was "Let your light so shine before men so that they may see your good works and glorify your Father which is in Heaven." The pastor at the time was Rev. N.N. Boles. In 2002, Rev. Gregory A. Tyson, Sr. became pastor. Under the leadership of Pastor Tyson, the church on 45th Street was completely renovated. In 2004, the church purchased property on ACL Blvd with plans of building a new house of worship. **On February 3, 2008** – the church celebrated and held its groundbreaking ceremony for the future home of our new church on ACL Blvd. **On December 13, 2008** – the congregation marched from their history on 219 West 45th Street into the church's future at 4370 ACL Blvd.

In 2011, the church purchased additional property on ACL Blvd adjacent to the church. During the same year, the church was also blessed with the purchase of two buses, known as Grace and Mercy. **Throughout the years** the church has been blessed with several youth ministries including but not limited to: The Gregory A. Tyson, Sr. Youth and Young Adult Choir, Boys II Men Ministries, S.I.S. Ministries, the TWIST Scholarship Ministry and Vacation Bible School. **On August 24, 2014,** the church was blessed as four elders and nine deacons were ordained.

On February 22, 2015, the Lord called Pastor Gregory A. Tyson Sr. home. During his 12 years as pastor, he had a tremendous impact on countless lives and was committed to the growth of the church, guided the youth in a special way and taught the word of God. His legacy in the community as well as in the church will live on forever.

Throughout 2015, the church spent several months in search of a new leader. In December 2015, Pastor Damion P. Gordon, Sr. was announced as the newly selected leader of the church. March 20, 2016, Pastor Gordon was installed as our new Pastor.

Today, First Jerusalem Missionary Baptist Church is committed to being a church of the Great Commandment and the Great Commission, empowering individuals to find their purpose in Christ.

FIRST EVERGREEN MISSIONARY BAPTIST CHURCH

Rev. Ronald B. Gregory, Pastor

First Evergreen Baptist Church was organized in 1900 on the corner of East Boundary and Wheaton Streets by Rev. C. L. Hayes. After being at this location for a short time, the members purchased a lot on East Gwinnett Street. In 1922 Rev. Hayes vacated the position for two years and Rev. Riley Mosely served. Rev. Hayes returned as pastor and served for 30 years. On June 22,1935, Rev. E.A. Capers, son of Evergreen, was named pastor. He served as Moderator of the Berean Missionary Baptist Association for thirty-three years. He retired on December 9,1977. In March 1978, Rev. Joe Frazier was named pastor. He served until his death on May 7, 1995. On September 15,1996, Rev. Leroy Jenkins was installed as pastor. Rev. Matthew Southall Brown, Sr. preached the Installation Sermon. Rev. Jenkins served until 2000. On July 20, 2000, Rev. Ronald Gregory, a son of the church, was installed as pastor. He is presently serving as pastor.

FIRST TABERNACLE MISSIONARY
BAPTIST CHURCH

Rev. Andre J. Osborne
Present Pastor

- The First Tabernacle Missionary Baptist Church was organized on October 16, 1898 under the Pastorate of Rev. J. C. Urby
- The original location of the Church was on Walker Street in Frog Town, Savannah, Georgia
- The Church has been relocated twice
- It was relocated to Huntington Street in 1903
- In 1914, it was relocated again to its current address, 310 Alice Street in Savannah
- The first brick was laid in 1913 by Sister Susan Exley, and the structure was completed in 1917

FORMER PASTORS
J. C. Urby (1898 - 1904)
Toby Sanford (1904 - 1906)
C. W. Carswell (1906 -1910)
E. D. Davis (1910 - 1944)
W. W. Wilburn (1944 - 1952)
Eugene Gates Lane (1952 -1967)
Samuel Williams (1968 - 1976)
W. N. Robinson (1977 - 1989)
H. Allen Green (1990 - 1996)
Paul L. Taylor (1997 - 2000)
Clarence Williams (2001 - Jan 5, 2014)
Marilyn L. Felder (Interim) (Jan - Oct 2014)

FIRST UNION MISSIONARY BAPTIST CHURCH

Organized in March 1890 in a place called "old Brick yard" on the west side of Savannah. Founder was Rev. Andrew Jackson and others.

The church moved to Steward Street. Members became dissatisfied and Rev. Jackson. He was replaced by Rev. Jack Thomas. A storm came through Savannah, and the church was damaged and later condemned by the city. The church was relocated on Charles Street in a four-room house. After a while Rev. Thomas was replaced by Rev. Woods.

Rev. Woods served for a short period of time and Rev. H. L. Howard of North Georgia. The membership grew and the Charles Street house became too small. Rev. James Moss was called to pastor the church. He only served a few months because of his declining health. Rev. Moss returned home to Augusta but died three weeks later. Rev. Williams, a faithful member and son of the church, was called to the pastorate, and later resigned.

In 1919 Rev. A.D. Dunbar was called to pastor. The church later moved to Jones Street with Dea. Golphin and Bennett spearheading the project.

Rev. Dunbar organized the Deaconess board in 1920. The senior choir was organized in 1922. In the meantime, the group that remained on Charles Street became discontent as well. One group eventually moved to Jones Street; one group remained on Charles Street. In 1927, the Charles Street group split and became known as Connor's Temple Baptist church; the Jones Street group remained as Union Baptist church, and the Charles Street group became Tremont Temple.

In 1941-Rev. Lucious C. Sapp became pastor (October 16, 1941). On February 18, 1945 the 535 Berrien Street building was dedicated. Rev. Sapp passed in 1961.

In Feb 1962 Rev. Pete Broxton became pastor. He ordained five sons into the ministry: Alton Anderson, Aaron Holmes, Japan Holmes, Willie Frank Stanley, Larry L. Broxton. Rev. Marvin Thompson and Rev. Clarence Boles came by Christian experience.

In 2002, Rev. Matthew S. Brown, Jr. was appointed to assist in pulpit services due to failing health of Pastor Broxton. In April 2003, Rev. Brown officially became pastor. Other ministers who were ordained were Revs. Alfreddie Mingledorff, Stanley Royal, Dennis Ceasar and Lou-Brown Epps. Rev. Brown embarked upon transitioning the church into the 21st century by incorporating technology into spreading the Word.

MOUNT ZION BAPTIST CHURCH

Mount Zion Baptist Church was established on November 22, 1876 in a framed house on Roberts Street in the Frogtown section of Savannah, Georgia. Three ordained ministers, John Habersham, A. Johnson and H.C. Aves along with Deacon Doc Williams formally organized the church. The name given to this new church was "Mount Zion Baptist Church."

Pastor Edward Brown was unanimously called as the first Pastor, and Brother H. King was elected as the first Clerk. The following Deacons were elected: John Judge, G. Heard, J. Howe, Thomas Anderson, S. Brooks, E. Warren and Sam Naylor. The Sunday School was organized with Brother Robert H. King as the first Superintendent. Pastor Edward T. Brown resigned the pastorate in February 1882. He served six years.

- 1882: A frame church on 512 West Broad (Martin Luther king, Jr, Blvd.) was purchased from the West Baptist Church for $1,100.
- 1883: ***Pastor W. L. P. Weston***, a minister from the White Bluff community was called by the church. During his ministry, there was a great religious awakening. Pastor Weston baptized 260 members in an 18 month period. He died in 1908.
- 1908: Pastor William McKinnie was called as the pastor. He served for eight months during which the church was wired for electricity and a pool was installed.
- 1910: Pastor Mac D. Spencer of Valdosta, Georgia was called to pastor Mt. Zion. During his pastorate, the 512 West Broad Street property was sold and the present place of worship, 1008 West Broad Street was purchased from the First Bryan Baptist Church. Pastor Spencer resigned in 1914.

- 1914: Church member, Pastor H.D. Butler, was called to serve as pastor of Mt. Zion. He served well until 1918 when he resigned to accept a church in the north.
- 1919: Reverend John Q. Adams was called as the pastor. He served for 59½ years during which time there was religious stability, material growth, building expansion and overall organizational development. During this time Pastor Adams missed only one communion service. He retired in 1978 and the congregation voted him the status of Pastor Emeritus.
- 1978: Pastor Jack DeLong Dash was called but the call was rescinded, and he was not installed.
- 1978: Pastor Robert Twyman of Detroit, Michigan was called and under his leadership many new ministries were organized as the church continued to progress. Pastor Twyman resigned in 1992.
- 1994: Pastor Clarence Boles, Jr. of Garland, Texas was called as the Pastor. During his ministry much of the infrastructure was updated and improved. Pastor Boles resigned in 1996
- 1999: Mount Zion Baptist Church elected Pastor Edward Carrol as pastor. During his pastorate the goal of greater involvement of the auxiliaries, departments and ministries was pursued with much success. Pastor Carroll resigned as minister of Mt. Zion in 2000 and relocated to the Atlanta area.
- 2002 to Present: The church called Pastor Michael S. Stamps, Sr. to be the minister. During his pastorate the church has been guided by the theme "Bible Based, Christ Center, Holy Spirit Led and Mission Bound." During this pastorate, many improvements have been made to the church and a great focus has been placed on outreach and evangelism.

Mount Zion continues to fellowship in the spirit of Christian love and service. Led by the anointed preaching of Pastor Stamps, the church body strives to study the Word and do good works. The past year was filled with activities that were designed to bring the brethren to Christ.

As this year ends and another year begins, we give God the Glory! We are grateful for His rich blessings upon us, and we celebrate our history with abiding love for our Redeemer, Jesus Christ, and one another. May we ever strive to "Build the Community as We Build the Kingdom".

RICHFIELD BAPTIST

Rev. Johnnie Powell

The Richfield Missionary Baptist Church was founded by Rev. Johnnie Powell and organized by Rev. J.M. Benton, Pastor of Tremont Temple Missionary Baptist Church of Savannah, on August 23,1968. The organization was in the Indepenent Christain Hall. Since that time the church membership has grown. The City of Savannah and Georgia Department of Inspection approved the construction of the present building at 1415 Arcadian Street. It was designed and built by Rev. Johnnie Powell.

Dedication Service was held on February 5,1984. Rev. George J. Faison, Pastor of Tremont Temple Missionary Baptist, delivered the dedication sermon. Several renovations were made to the church to include restrooms, handicap ramp, carpet, and in 1996, the Fellowship Hall was added.

SECOND ST. JOHN MISSIONARY BAPTIST CHURCH

Second Saint John Missionary Baptist Church was organized April 15, 1917 by Reverend J. J. Johnson with a small band of six members. The church was originally in Collat Quarters, Savannah, Georgia. We began worshipping in our current edifice on January 22, 1961. We have had several pastors to lead our congregation. Our current pastor, Pastor Marques C. Johnson Sr., a pastor after God's own heart, is currently leading us to a higher spiritual calling where the pieces are coming together. Our church has several ministries including a dynamic G.A.N.G. (God's Anointed New Generation) Youth Ministry witnessing through nonverbal communications. Our Library/Resource Center, named for the late Mother Ernestine Manigault, is located on the second floor in the Educational Building.

History as taken from the church website

PILGRIM OF SAVANNAH

Rev. Dr. Clarence Williams, Jr.

PASTOR

From Savannah's rich history of African American Churches comes the name "Pilgrim Baptist Church". The Savannah Tribune records 1915 as the year "Pilgrim Baptist Church" was founded in Savannah, Georgia. On January 12, 2014, Rev. Clarence Williams, Jr. organized Pilgrim Baptist Church of Savannah. First Pilgrim Missionary Baptist Church is the church where Williams was licensed and ordained. Since then, First Pilgrim Missionary Baptist Church has dissolved and Williams is now carrying the name "Pilgrim" into a new era of Christian fellowship and ministries.

He is the nineth moderator of the Berean Missionary Baptist Association, Inc. and former Vice President of the National Baptist Convention, USA, Inc. Music Auxiliary. He serves on a number of community boards and is a certified instructor in Christian Education.

Second African Baptist Church

The records of the Second African Baptist Church, Savannah, Georgia are divided into seven series: Church Minutes; Legal Documents; Church Rolls, Minute Books and Annual Reports; Financial Records; Sunday School Records, Church Organizations' Minutes; and Church History, Printed Matter, Miscellaneous.

BIOGRAPHICAL/HISTORICAL INFORMATION

Second African Baptist Church was founded in 1802 by members of the First Colored Church (now the First African Baptist Church of Savannah). In the early years of the 19th century, the Savannah River Association, an organization of Baptist churches composed of one black and two white Baptist churches: The First Colored Church (black), the Newington Baptist Church and the Savannah Baptist Church, decided to strengthen the Association by organizing two additional black churches out of the membership of the First Colored Church which at the time had a membership of 850. The two black churches which were formed were Second Colored Church and the Ogeechee Baptist Church. Two hundred members were dismissed from the First Colored Church and joined with the African Americans who had been members in the white Savannah Baptist Church to constitute Second Colored Church.

Two African American ministers were ordained to serve the new churches. Rev. Henry Cunningham, a former slave, became the first pastor of Second Colored Church and served for thirty-one years from 1802 to 1833.

The founding members of Second Colored Church were described as intelligent and industrious. Most of them worked as domestic servants or mechanics and lived in the area where the church was located. Many members who were slaves followed the example of their pastor and later purchased their freedom.

After its founding, Second Colored Church continued to have a close relationship with the First Colored Church. Following the death of Andrew Bryan, the second pastor of the First Colored Church, Second Colored Church furnished, in regular succession, pastors for the First Colored or mother church from 1812 to 1846.

The first of the pastors that went to First Colored Church from Second Colored Church was Andrew Cox Marshall in 1815. Rev. Marshall had joined Second Colored Church after he had been baptized by Rev. Cunningham.

In 1823 the First Colored Church and the Second Colored Church were renamed First African Baptist Church and Second African Baptist Church respectively by the Sunbury Association which had replaced the Savannah River Association.

The second pastor of Second African Baptist Church was Thomas Anderson. Rev. Anderson, one of the organizers of the original Second Colored Church, had been baptized by Andrew Bryan. In 1833, he was called to pastor the Third Colored Church, later renamed First Bryan Baptist Church, when it split from First African Baptist Church in that same year. Anderson pastored the newly constituted church then known as the Third African Baptist Church. After two years, in 1835, Anderson returned to Second African Baptist Church where he served until 1849.

- Rev. John Cox, 1849-1871.
- Rev. H.L. Simpson, 1871-1881
- Rev. Alexander Ellis, 1883-1889. During his administration, the church was remodeled. In 1889 Rev. Ellis was deposed following a disagreement between himself and members of the choir. A council of three white ministers met and rendered a decision which was not acceptable to Rev. Ellis. An election was held on December 13, 1889 and Ellis was deposed as pastor. Ellis and his supporters then formed Beth Eden Baptist Church.
- ***Rev. J. J. Durham, 1891-1902. Final payment for the remodeling of the church was made during his tenure. One of the original members in July 1899***
- Rev. John H. May 1903-1907.
- Rev. S. H. Smith, 1907. He only served six months during which time he suffered a stroke and had to resign.
- Rev. Ira De Reid or D. A. Reid, 1908-1914. He was a native of the West Indies. A pipe organ was installed and the church was renovated during his administration.
- Rev. W. Boliver Davis, 1915-1918
- Rev. P. W. Wrenn, 1919-1922.
- Rev. S. D. Ross, 1923-1928. Rev. Ross organized the church into fifteen departments. The church building was completely renovated following a fire in 1926.

- Rev. Miles A. Hunter, 1929-1931.
- Rev. Clifton Norman Perry, 1931-1934. Rev. Perry was noted as a good gospel preacher.
- Rev. Ivory W. Collins, 1935-1937. While serving as a waiter at the DeSoto Hotel, Ivory W. Collins was selected as a supply minister. It was noted that although he did not have the training of previous pastors he had a natural gift and talent for the ministry. Rev. Collins was later accepted as pastor and served two years. He left to continue his studies in the ministry.
- Rev. C. L. Hawk, 1938-1942
- Rev. Lewis Llewellyn Scott, 1942-1949
- Rev. Edgar Perry Quarterman, 1947-1983. During Rev. Quarterman's tenure, the church was renovated and a heating and cooling system installed.
- Rev. James H. Cantrell, 1983-Present (1997)

ST. JOHN THE MIGHTY FORTRESS

In 1885, the east side of Savannah, Georgia was lacking in opportunities to affiliate as a faith community, which is necessary to the fulfillment of a good Christian life. Through the divine providence of Almighty God, one of His chosen few, Reverend William Gray, was anointed to fill the void in religiosity. Father Gray, a member of the historic First Bryan Baptist Church, sought and obtained the permission and blessing of First Bryan, to start a church on the east side. Reverend Gray established the St. John Baptist Church in 1885. The congregation of former slaves erected the original church building at 526-28 Hartridge Street, in July 1891.

A terrible fire on October 24, 1993 destroyed the original building. Initially, the congregation was overwhelmed by the devastation, but soon realized, as Pastor Brown said, "After all, the church is really not brick and mortar, but the church is people." Thereafter, St. John dedicated itself to the continued uplifting of God's kingdom on earth, wherever they worshipped. Their place of worship while the new "Mighty Fortress" rose from the ashes, was the West Broad Street Seventh Day Adventist Church. The situation revealed the ability of God's children to worship under the same roof, regardless of denomination.

St. John has had only five pastors since its inception:

Father Gray; 1885 - 1926
Rev. E.O.S. Cleveland 1927-1963
Rev. Cameron Alexander 1965-1969
Rev. Matthew Southall Brown 1969-2004
Rev. George P. Lee III, Ph.D. 2005 -Present

TREMONT TEMPLE MISSIONARY BAPTIST CHURCH

Tremont Temple Missionary Baptist Church began with a series of prayer meetings that were held in the homes of the original twenty-two members. The group moved from the homes to one room in the Masonic Temple located at 511 West Gwinnett Street. This was the beginning of the group that became known as the Tremont Temple Baptist Church on April 22, 1922. Father Gray served as moderator in the calling of Rev. J. L. Dudley as the church's first Pastor. The members voted to purchase a two (2) unit family dwelling on the corner of Park Lane and West Broad Street and remodeled the dwelling to become the official place of worship.

The second Pastor, Rev. Dinkins, directed the Trustees to proceed in acquiring a grocery store and two rental houses next to the Church due to the church's financial growth. His vision was to build a bigger and better Church edifice. He completed his workday on earth at the age of 53.

The third Pastor, Reverend Jeremiah Benton, immediately guided the officers of the church to secure a permit from the city to begin construction of the present edifice. Rev. Benton guided the membership and officers in managing and paying the debt for the new edifice and an educational building with a Fellowship Hall was added to the main sanctuary.

The fourth Pastor, Rev. George J. Faison, Sr., led the congregation in the expansion of the church with an annex that contained a state of the art Learning Center, offices, and expansion of the Fellowship Hall in 1987. The church increased its possessions for additional expansions with the purchase of property by the fifth and present Pastor.

The church grew to approximately 725 members, and God is still blessing us. During the past 94 years God has blessed us with six dynamic leaders:

> Rev. James Lee Dudley, 1922-1926
> Rev. Rufus James Dinkins, 1926-1946
> Rev. Jeremiah Matthew Benton, 1946-1973
> Rev. George James Faison, 1974-2000
> Rev. Ricky Alan Bready, Sr., 2001-2011
> Rev. Quentin J. Morris, Sr., 2012-Present

IVY RICHARDSON'S CONCLUSION

Why church history? I cannot answer that question for the Historian, Dea. Johnnie P. Jones, and the History Committee's members of 2000. I never sat in the History Committee's meetings, for I joined and attended the Association's meetings in 2012. But I am aware that the collection of each church's history was a component of the Committee's report by Dea. Jones.

So once again I say, "A charge to keep I have to serve the present age in whose hands this book now holds." Dea. Jones began with a collection of materials, but he couldn't get beyond those five pages as presented to [me by] his wife. I couldn't get past the initial pages as presented to Rev. Matthew Southall Brown, Sr. because God's spark pushed me past the limitations of each church history to one church. Why First African Baptist of Darien, Georgia? Now, you see fifty-one churches in the Association. You read the writer's commentary on study as Paul taught in the Marketplace of Brea. Did you link it to those Pastors' presence in the church on Market Street?

And so, on behalf of Dea. Jones, the History Committee, and our heavenly Father's spark, this book is rendered to the Berean Association. I pray the desires of the committee are one day filled in the second edition for future generations to read. Also, I pray, the fifty-one churches make it easy for future generations to search their church's records as placed on disk and recorded in Mercer University Library's files in Macon, Georgia.

Then, Beth Eden Baptist Church members will know that Rev. Nathaniel MacPherson Clarke served on the Executive Board for the Berean Missionary Baptist Association. First Bryan Baptist Church will know the centennial celebration of one hundred (100) years for the Berean Missionary Baptist Association was celebrated October 6-8 of 1999 at their church. They [All Bereans] will know the significance of education as they read about the Savannah City Directory's 1925 to 1927 listing of the Berean Baptist Association's operation of a Nursery and kindergarten and its closing in 1935.

Above all, I pray that today's generation comes to see that their ordeals of life are just a prayer away. God has their "This".

BIBLIOGRAPHY

Bell, Malcolm. Major's Butler's Legacy: Five Generations of A Slave Holding Family. pg. 554.

Brawley, Benjamin. The Project Gutenberg eBook of A Social History of the American Negro.

Bunyan, Arthur (2016) History of the American Negro, Vol. 2: Georgia Edition, 1920.

Garner, Robert (2012) Georgia Baptist Association And Convention Records. 1733-2010

Martin, Sandy D. (1998) Black Baptists and African Missions: The Origins of a Movement, 1880-1955.

National Advancement for Colored People's document of lynching in the United States.

Negro Education: A Study of the Private and Higher Schools for Colored People", Volume 2, Pg250

Severance, Diane. Church Timelines.

Wagner. (1980) Berean Baptist Association C 1899; African American; active.

> Boxed: 1919 Reel 1371: 1909 [ABHS] AUC: 1915-1942 (with gaps); SS, 1916-1931

Wells, Ida B. (1899) "Lynch Law in Georgia," (Chicago: Chicago Colored Citizens, 1899)

The Berean Example, Forerunner's, November 2000 edition.

> http://www.thebereanassociation.org/
> http://www.cityofdarienga.com
> http://firstafricanbc.com
> http://www.firstjerusalem.org/about_us.php
> http://www.glynngen.com/index.html
> http://www.glynngen.com/index.html:Pg 3, Col,3
> http://www.pbs.org/wgbh/amex/till/peopleevents/e_lynch.html
> http://www.savannahtribune.com/articles

Part II

CHAPTER I

THE FOUNDATION

Sis. Ivy Richardson, author of Part I, identified the Berean Association Moderators to Moderator Clarence Williams, Jr. Part II adds more insight not only to tenures of Moderators Matthew Southall Brown, Sr., and Moderator Clarence Williams, Jr. but also Moderator Richard L. Hall, Sr., Moderator Andre J. Osborne, meetings, sessions, Annual Sessions, Adjourned Sessions, and missing moments in history.

The website 2023, bereanmba.org, designed and maintained by Minister Johnnie Perkins, gives insight into the Berean Missionary Baptist Association today with the focus on equipping, edifying, exalting, and evangelizing with the general mission of Building Healthy Churches. The website lists the goals, benefits, the description of the New Testament Model upon which the Association must continue, and a closing comment by former Moderator, Dr. Richard L. Hall, Sr. (2019-2021):

GOAL

The goal of this association is to "Build Healthy Churches" and maintain the health of the church through EQUIPPING ministries, EDIFYING members, and EXALTING Christ through EVANGELISM. **Thematic Scripture:** *"And he gave the apostles, the prophets, the evangelists, the shepherds and teachers, to equip the saints for the work of ministry, for building up the body of Christ" (Ephesians 4:11-12 ESV).*

THE BENEFITS OF BEING A BEREAN ASSOCIATION CHURCH

"What we have is well designed and biblically sound!"

Nothing exceeds the joys and benefits that we have by being part of the Berean Association of Churches. **Acts 17:11** is the model passage for this association... *"they received the word with all readiness, and searched the Scriptures daily to find out whether these things were so."*

PERSONAL BENEFITS

On an individual level, the Berean sessions are joyful reminders of the many friendships we have made with pastors and churches over the years. We enjoy these friendships built around a common faith, worship, and activities that the Association provides. *"Continue in brotherly love" (Hebrews 13:1).*

CHILDREN'S BENEFITS

I'm well aware that parents are to teach their children. *"Train up a child in the way he should go, and when he is old, he will not depart from it" (Proverbs 22:6).* Teach children how they should live, and they will remember it all their life.

We are also strong believers in the statement that it takes a "Village" to raise a child, and we believe a network of churches will help get the job done. We shouldn't trust just anyone to do the job, nor trust just any curriculum that has the word "youth" in it. We simply cannot trust the care of our children to anybody.

We want people and ministries that will reinforce the teachings and values of the Christian home. The Berean Association provides the ministries that children can trust. This association is led by godly adults and young adults who love God and children. This association, we believe, is of unlimited value to our children.

FAMILY BENEFITS

"Fathers, do not provoke your children to anger; instead, bring them up in the discipline and instruction of the Lord" (Ephesians 6:4). Our parents are encouraged and strengthened when they can load our children into a van and send them to youth rallies sponsored by the Berean Association. The rally may be a gathering at a building outside of a church building, but we are confident that our children will receive preaching, teaching, and activities consistent with the convictions and values of our association.

We send our children with confidence, knowing that they will be challenged; some will get saved; all will be confronted with the Word of God to live godly lives in an ungodly world.

None of our churches on its own could manage and operate a ministry of this size and capability, but together we can. Our families and churches are strengthened through this remarkable connection of churches.

CHURCH BENEFITS

"For as we have many members in one body, but all the members do not have the same functions" Romans 12:4).

Benefits of our association are numerous and marvelous. The ordination for the gospel ministry is an extremely important function of the church. To gather a committee of trusted leaders from Association churches to help examine the candidate for their doctrinal belief is wise and helpful. And when churches find themselves involved in struggles that they seemingly cannot resolve, it is of great benefit to engage the help of wise, impartial people of churches like their own. Unfortunately, this practice is probably not made use of as often as it should be.

When receiving potential new members of the church, a pastor should make it a practice to call the former church. He or she could discover where the prospects are spiritually, so the transition can be effective in guiding them to spiritual maturity. The pastor may also discover that a prospect is running from discipline or is constantly dissatisfied.

A church without a pastor often reaches out to an association representative for help. The representative will not just give the church a list of names but will counsel the church search committee concerning the process and help them make wise informed decisions concerning a potential shepherd for their church. Churches can benefit greatly from checking out prospects with coworkers in sister churches to determine their reputations. All these services are available when requested.

NEW TESTAMENT MODEL

Much has changed in the last two thousand years, but the New Testament gives us examples of churches that banded together to solve a doctrinal conflict or to help a church in desperate financial difficulty due to a natural disaster or persecution. Churches at that early stage did not have an official association of churches. But it was natural and helpful for them to work together for the purpose of strengthening and advancing the cause of Christ. Christians personally, and churches collectively, benefited.

To me, the benefits of being in an association of churches of like faith and practice has not diminished but rather has increased. I am personally grateful for the association I have and that our church has in the Berean Association. The older I get, the longer I pastor, and the more I think about it, I realize that what connects us is greater than what separates us... Immediate Past Moderator, Dr. Richard L. Hall, Sr.,2019-2021 ("Our Goal").

CHAPTER II

THE HISTORICAL PERSPECTIVE

Sessions

The Annual Sessions meet to handle the business of the Berean Missionary Baptist Association, Inc. The Adjourned Sessions meet to handle the unfinished business of the Annual Sessions and to move forward with the year's calendar. However, periods of history make references to meetings, sessions, annual sessions, and adjourned sessions.

The Mother Association _ Zion Association

Zion Missionary Baptist Association is the oldest Negro Association in North American, and from this association, many other associations were organized, including the Berean Missionary Baptist Association, Inc. "This historical body was founded by our forefathers on Christian principles for the purpose of bringing together the Negro Baptist Churches. This Association was composed of churches from South Carolina, Georgia, and Florida (Zion Missionary Baptist Association).

The great men who were present to ensure the organization of Zion Missionary Baptist Association were Rev. U.L. Houston, Deacon A. Harris, Bro. S. Whitehead, Bro. A Bourke, Bro. W.J. Campbell, Bro. A Mercherson, Bro. J. Jones, Rev. Andrew Neal, Rev. Daniel Curry, Rev. Wm. Morrison, and Rev. J. M. Sims. Rev. U.L. Houston was chosen chairman (Zion Missionary Baptist Association).

Four churches from Savannah, Ga were present. These churches were members of the Sunbury Association (white) and three churches of Beaufort District, S.C. were constituted [organized] during the war. Rev. John Cox, Pastor of the Second African Baptist Church, Savannah, was elected Moderator of the Association, Bro. K. S. Thomas, clerk; Rev. U.L. Houston, Treasurer. Rev. Houston preached the opening sermon (Zion Missionary Baptist Association).

In July 1866, the Zion Association was held in Savannah, GA at F.A.B.C. [First African Baptist Church], the oldest Negro Church in North America. Rev. A. Rourke was elected Moderator. The following members of committee drafted the Constitution: A. Harris, A. Bourke, W.J. Campbell, A. Mercherson, and J. Jones (Zion Missionary Baptist Association).

At the Association meeting July 1872, F.A.B.C. in Darien, GA, Rev. U.L. Houston, 9th Pastor of Bryan B.C., Savannah, GA, was elected Moderator (Zion Missionary Baptist Association).

An Offspring _ The Berean Missionary Baptist Association

According to the *Savannah Tribune:*

Berean Association – More than one hundred delegates of the Zion Association met at Mt. Zion Church, in this city, last Wednesday to consider the organization [of the Berean Association] of another organization. After due consideration it was voted to organize under the name the "Berean Association". Officers elected were Rev. W. L. P. Weston, Moderator [See Part I: the second Moderator for the Berean Missionary Baptist Association and the first Moderator for the city of Savannah], Rev. E.M. Brawley, D.D., Secretary; Rev. R. H. Thomas, Treasurer. The body then adjourned to meet in its first annual session at Zion White Bluff Church, Thursday before the third Lord's Day in July 1900 *(Savannah Tribune* 12 Aug. 1899, 2*).*

The Zion Missionary Baptist Association History states:

In July1899, the Association was held with F.A.B Church Dari [Darien], Ga. Rev. P.R. Mifflin, pastor. In June 1899, before the Association met, the treasurer, Rev. Wm. Morrison, was called by death. This was a year of unrest. It seemed as though the main objective was office seeking. Rev. S. Beauford, who was Moderator, was succeeded by the late Rev. P.J. Butler. It was after the adjournment of this session that the Revs. J.J. Durham, S. Beauford, R. H. Thomas, and others organized the Berean Association (Zion Missionary Baptist Association).

The Berean Missionary Baptist Association with Moderator P. J. Butler began with the guiding thought of study. "Study to shew thyself approved unto God, a workman that needeth not to be ashamed, rightly dividing the word of truth," 2 Timothy 2:15. Who are the Bereans? Act 17:10-12 indicates the Bereans' character as they "examine the scriptures daily to see if what Paul and Silas preached was so ("Bereans in the Bible").

CHAPTER III

THE BEREAN ASSOCIATION
1900 – 1960

A description of the Sunday School Convention follows:

The Sunday School Convention of the Berean Association will meet with the College Park Sunday School, beginning August 31. Delegates who will attend are requested to send their names to Mr. R.H. Thomas at College, GA, so that homes will be prepared for them (*Savannah Tribune* 11 Aug. 1900, 3).

The Berean Sunday School Convention was organized on August 31, 1900, at College Park Baptist Church, Rev. R.H. Thomas, Pastor. Officers elected were President and Secretary Pro Tempore, Rev. Hosea Maxwell and Mrs. Hanshaw. The convention breathed the first breath of its new existence under the presidency of Rev. R.H. Thomas. His associates were as follows:

Rev. S. Beauford, Waycross, GA; M. S. Grant, Darien, GA (Secretary); Mrs. Mary M. Miller, Savannah, GA (Treasurer); Mrs. M. M. Monroe, Savannah, GA (Auditor); and Mrs. L. Lewis, Darien, GA (Auditor) (*Savannah Tribune* 15 Sept. 1900, 3*)*.

Plans made for travel to the Berean Association:

An excursion will be given to Darien, via S.A.L. on Sunday, July 28; for the convenience of all who wish to attend the Berean Baptist Association which convenes beginning Thursday the 25th. Trains leave Central Depot at 5 a.m. and arrive at 7:30 a.m., and leave Darien 8:30 p.m. Fare round trip - $1.00 (*Savannah Tribune* 20 July 1901, 3).

The Berean Baptist Association is holding its annual meeting at Darien beginning Thursday. Among those in attendance are Revs. J.J. Durham, D.D. Alex Harris, G.W. Griffin, Rev. R.H. Thomas, Rev. W.L.P. Weston. Deacons W.R. Fields, W.A. Houston and others (*Savannah Tribune* 27 July1901, 3).

The writer notes an interesting Berean Association Session:

The second annual session of the Berean Baptist Association met at the Grace Baptist Church, Darian, Georgia [Darien] on Thursday of last week. The Introductory Sermon was preached by Rev. W.H. Anderson. The following officers were elected: President, Rev. W.L.P. Weston, Savannah, GA; Vice

President, Rev. J.J. Durham, D.D., Savannah, GA; Secretary, Rev. Samuel Beauford, Waycross, GA; Treasurer, Rev. R.H. Thomas, College, GA. The Executive Board met and was organized with Rev. Alexander Harris, Chairman and Rev. Beauford, Secretary (*Savannah Tribune* 3 Aug. 1901, 2).

All the Baptist Churches with 2 exceptions are represented at the meeting of the Berean Baptist Association in Waycross (*Savannah Tribune* 26 July1902, 3).

The Union meeting of the Berean Baptist Association will be held on the 5th Sunday at Montgomery Baptist Church. Rev. J.W. Hill, Pastor (*Savannah Tribune*, Aug. 1902).

Rev. T.M. Williamson, B.D. has returned from Waycross where he has been attending the Berean Association on last Sunday; at 11a.m. he preached the Missionary Sermon which made a lasting impression on the vast audience (*Savannah Tribune*, 2 Aug 1902, 3).

The Sunday School Convention of the Berean Association were [was] to have held its Annual Session at Bloomingdale, bet [but] for prudential reasons it is holding its Convention at St. John Baptist Church in this city. There will be a mass meeting of all Sunday School workers to which the public is invited (*Savannah Tribune* 23 Aug. 1902).

Additional information on the Berean Baptist Sunday School continues:

The Berean Baptist Sunday School Convention convened at Darien, GA last week in the 2nd African Baptist Church, Friday morning, the president, Rev. R.H. Thomas, called the body to order. Officers were elected as follows: Rev. R.H. Thomas, College, GA, President; Rev. H.L. Haywood, Savannah, Vice President; L.G. Fleming, Savannah, Recording Secretary; J.H. Moultrie, Corresponding Secretary; Mrs. M.M. Mills, Savannah, Treasurer; L.D. Lewis, Darien, and Miss Harriet Delegall, Harris Neck, auditors; and a Finance Committee consisting of Miss. Carrie B. Hendrickson and Messrs. R.M. Davis and C.F. Waters (*Savannah Tribune*, 29 Aug.1903, 2).

Rev. W.L.P. Weston described in Part I as the second Moderator, the *Savannah Tribune* gives more insight into the man:

W.L.P. Weston ... is next to the oldest Minister in the city. He was born in Virginia, about 75 years ago and has been a Georgian about half a century, during a greater part of which he has been identified with the Ministry. He was ordained at 1st Bryan B.C. of which Rev. U.L. Houston was the pastor at the time. His first charge was the church at White Bluff. ... About twenty-three years ago he was called to the pastorate of the Mt. Zion B.C. His work has been a successful one. He is the Beloved Moderator of the Berean Baptist Association, one of the largest bodies in the state. ... He is upright in all of his dealings and is a true believer in a "Clean Pulpit" in every respect (*Savannah Tribune* 4 Feb.1905, 5).

Listed are more sessions and meetings of the Berean Baptist Association:

The Berean Baptist Association is in session at Bethlehem Baptist Church (*Savannah Tribune* 22 July 1905).

An excursion will be run to Harris Neck to meet the Berean Baptist Association, by Zion White Bluff B.C., leaving Saturday night, July 21, 9 o'clock. Fare $1.00 (*Savannah Tribune* 7 July 1906, 5).

The Sixth Annual Session of the Berean Association Sunday School was held with the Elm Grove Baptist School at McIntosh County, Ga last week, and by far it was the most successful session held by the body (*Savannah Tribune* 1 Sept.1906).

The Berean Baptist Association commenced its Eighth Annual Session at St. John B.C., Rev. Wm. Gray, pastor, on Thursday morning. The session will continue until Sunday. Nearly all the Baptist Churches in the city are members of this Association and it has among its membership some of the leading Baptist divines [divine leaders] in the state (*Savannah Tribune* 27 July1907, 4).

Officers for the ensuing year: Rev. Wm. Gray, Moderator; Rev. M. Williamson, Vice Moderator, Waycross; Rev. H.L. Haywood, Secretary; Dea. E.W. Thorpe, Treasurer, Lacy, GA. This Session was harmonious. The Associational Sermons delivered by Revs. T.M. Williamson, R.G. Carter, H.L. Haywood, and J.H. May, D.D., were said to be masterpieces. The next session will be held at Waycross (*Savannah Tribune* 3 Aug. 1907, 5).

The Berean Baptist Sunday School Convention will convene at Union B.C. at 10 O'clock on Friday next (*Savannah Tribune* 17 Aug. 1907, 5).

Morning Star Baptist Church, Rev. H.L. Haywood, Pastor
Our church was inducted into the Berean Association at the board meeting, and we invite all sister churches to be a part of this group (*Savannah Tribune* 13 June 1908, 4).

The delegates to the Sunday School Convention of the Berean Baptist Association which meets in Darien on the 21st are informed that there will be a special coach via Seaboard Air Line [which] will leave Savannah at 2:05 p.m. (Railroad Time) on Thursday August 20th. A rate of 2 cents per mile as far as Darien Junction. All delegates, Sunday School workers, and friends intending to go will be governed accordingly. Rev.

R.H. Thomas, president and J.E. Miller, Secretary (*Savannah Tribune* 15 Aug.1908, 4).

The Tenth Annual Session of the Berean Baptist Association met at the Abercorn Baptist Church near Exley, GA, July 22nd – 25th. The church is located in a pretty grove near the river. The session was considered one of the most successful ever held. Officers: Rev. Wm. Gray, Moderator; Rev. J.H. May, Vice Moderator; Rev. I.J. Yancy, Secretary; Rev. D.D. Mills, Treasurer (*Savannah Tribune* 31 July1909, 4).

The Woman's Auxiliary was organized at Waycross, Georgia last year. Officers: Mrs. M.M. Mills, President; Mrs. C. Sims, Vice President; Mrs. E.R. Dennis, Secretary; Mrs. Brown, Treasurer. *Savannah Tribune* 31 July1909, 4).

The next session of the association will meet with the White Oak Baptist Church, Monteith, Georgia, Rev. Moody, pastor (*Savannah Tribune* 31 July1909, 4).

"Study to show thyself approved a workman unto God," a mantra of the Berean Association, the Association held a Board Meeting of the Berean Baptist Academy:

On September 9th -12th the Trustee Board of the Berean Baptist Academy met at St. John B.C. Rev. Wm. Gray, D.D., Pastor. Rev. H.L. Haywood was elected Chairman; Rev. H.W. Williams, Secretary; Rev. A. J. Frazier, Treasurer; Rev. McD.

Spencer, Chairman of the auditing committee; Rev. Wm. Gray, Chairman of the Advisory Committee; Rev. Wm. Dun was elected president of the Berean Baptist Academy, this city. The Berean Baptist Academy will open Wednesday October 13, 1912. All Churches and Pastors of The Berean Baptist Association are asked to come and bring a donation for said school. Send all money for the school to Rev. A.J. Frazier, 112 Gordon St. Lane E., Savannah, Ga. (*Savannah Tribune* 21Sept. 1912, 4.)

The Berean Baptist Association Adds New Churches:

The 14th Session held at St. John B.C. Rev. Wm. Gray, reelected Moderator – Total of 30 Delegates present – Four lots purchased for erection of school – Over $750.00 raised. There were delegates from all the churches of the Association, the total being 300 of this number the Women's Auxiliary sent 120. Rev. Wm. Gray was reelected Moderator, Rev. L. Bond was elected 1st Vice Moderator, Rev. M. Burk, 2nd Vice Moderator and Rev. R.G. Carter, Clerk. Treasurer and Missionary, Rev. D.D. Mils and Rev. J.R. Maxwell were respectively elected. Five new churches were added to the Association (*Savannah Tribune* 2 Aug. 1913, 1).

A number of Missionary Clubs and Children's Bands were well represented by sending not less than four delegates. The

Auxiliary has taken on new life under the leadership of Mrs. E.R. Dennis, President. $210.76 was raised by the Auxiliary, $75.00 was presented to the Association Sunday night. The Officers are Mrs. E.R. Dennis, President; Miss. A.E. Maxwell, Recording Secretary; Mrs. M.S. Grant, Corresponding Secretary; Miss. A.J. Brown, Treasurer (*Savannah Tribune* 9 Aug.1913, 4).

Large Delegation Present at the Berean Association:

The Berean Baptist Association Convened at Central Baptist Church, Thunderbolt GA, Rev. D.D. Mills, Pastor on July 23rd -26th. The Session was a success in every way. The Session ended on Thursday morning with Rev. Wm. Gray, Pastor of St. John Baptist Church as Moderator.

cont.

While the male delegates were holding their session at Central Baptist Church, the Women's Auxiliary under the presidency of Mrs. Emma Dennis was holding its session at the white Methodist church at Thunderbolt.

cont.

During the entire session of the Association, complete harmony prevailed. Sixty-three churches and about 40 Sunday Schools were represented. Among the many interesting [things] of the Association was the great interest in the support and the enlargement of the Berean Baptist Academy. Rev. Wm. Gray, President, Rev. Wm. Durden, Chairman of the Board of Trustees, Miss. Alice Brown, Principal.

cont.

During last year, over 300 pupils were enrolled. The Association voted that October 7th next year be known as Berean Baptist Academy Rally Day. Each of the 11,575 delegates was asked to pay 25¢ for the support of the school (*Savannah Tribune* 1 Aug. 1914, 1).

Berean Association Meets in Waycross:

The Berean Association and [Baptist Young People's Union] B.Y.P.U. of the Baptist Churches met at the 1st African Baptist Church, Waycross, GA on Thursday of last week in one of the best sessions of the association. There were about 100 delegates present with this city leading in the number of representatives. The Berean Association met Thursday with Mrs. M.A. Grant of Waycross presiding. Rev. Wm. Gray delivered the principal sermon, being assisted by H.D. Butler, also of this city. Rev. R.H. Thomas presided at the meeting on Friday, which all the old officers were selected. The Joint Meeting was adjourned Sunday night, to meet next year at Daufuskie Island, S.C., the second Thursday in August 1915. The Officers of the B.Y.P.U. [Baptist Young People Union] of the Berean Association are: Mrs. M.S. Grant, President; Mr. G.W. Jones, Vice President; Miss A.E. Maxwell, Recording Secretary; Mrs. A.I. Rivers, Treasurer; Mrs. M.E. Burns, Corresponding Secretary. The Officers of the Sunday School Convention are: R.H. Thomas, Rev. I.J. Yancy, Vice President; Mrs. J.C. Woodruff, Recording Secretary; Rev. A.L. Hamilton, Corresponding Secretary; Mr. D. Simmons, Treasurer; Auditors: Mrs. M.S. Grant and Miss. L.E. Hendrickson (*Savannah Tribune* 15 August 1914, 1.)

The Berean Baptist Association is in session here and will close tomorrow night. The Officers elected are Rev. Wm. Gray, Moderator; Rev. L. Bond, Vice Moderator; Rev. D. Wright, Treasurer; Rev. R.G. Carter, Clerk (*Savannah Tribune* 24 July 1915, 1).

The Annual Session of the Berean Baptist Association is being held at Waycross. The Women's Auxiliary of the association is holding its session at the same time. Rev. Wm. Gray, D.D., is the Moderator, and Rev. A.R. Stalling [Starling] is the pastor of the church where the session is being held (*Savannah Tribune* 15 July1916, 1.)

The Berean Baptist Association Convention convened here in its Seventeenth Annual Session at 1st African Baptist Church, at 10 O'clock this morning. Rev. A.R. Starling,

Pastor, Rev. Wm. Gray, of Savannah, Moderator, presided. The Introductory Sermon was preached by Rev. R.H. Thomas of Savannah. The Moderator delivered his annual address. Following the address, the rule was suspended, and he was elected to succeed himself, unanimously, also the old [remaining] officers as follows: Rev. Wm. Gray, Moderator, Savannah, GA; Rev. L. Bond, Vice Moderator, Savannah. GA; R.G. Carter, Clerk, Darien, GA; Rev. Daniel Wright, Treasurer, Savannah, GA; Rev. J.W. Edwards, Missionary, Savannah; Rev. A.L. Hamilton, School Agent, Savannah, GA. *(Savannah Tribune* 22 July1916, 1).

"Study to show thyself approved a workman unto God," the Berean Academy Opens October 2nd:

To whom it may concern: This is to certify that Berean Baptist Academy will open October 2, 1916, at the corner of Waters Avenue and Wheaton Street, with Miss Alice Brown, principal. All members and friends in and out of the bounds of the Berean Association are requested to send their children and also be present on the opening day. Board of Directors: Rev. A. Wilder, Rev. I.W. Washington, Rev. L.J. Biggins, Rev. R.J. Kelly, Rev. J.H. Edwards, Rev. J.W. Edwards, Rev. W.H. Prince, Rev. H.D. Butler, Rev. Wm. Gray. Officers: Rev.

J.J. Erly, D.D., President; J.H. White, Treasurer; J.S. Moody, Secretary (*Savannah Tribune* 7 Oct. 1916, 7).

Berean Ministers, Sessions, and Women's Home Mission suggests fruitful years for the Berean Baptist Association:

The Ministers of the Berean Baptist Association will hold a meeting next Wednesday, May 22nd, at 2nd Pilgrim Baptist Church, Rev. R. H. Simmons, pastor, 513 East Bay Street. Rev. Wm. Gray is Moderator of the Association and expects a large attendance of the ministers (*Savannah Tribune* 18 May1918,1).

The Berean Baptist Association held its Eighteenth Annual Session at St. John B.C. last week. One of the best sessions in the history of the organization was experienced by the large delegation. All officers were reelected as follows: Rev. Wm. Gray, Moderator; Rev. L. Bond, Vice Moderator; Rev. B.G. Carter, Clerk; Rev. Daniel Wright, Treasurer; Rev. J.W. Edwards, Missionary. The Association reported $1,093.09 raised during the year (*Savannah Tribune* 3 Aug. 1918, 7).

The Women's Auxiliary of the Berean Baptist Association convened Thursday July 24th at [St. John] John B.C., Savannah. The meeting was called to order by the president. A number of delegates were present from Waycross, Darien, Monteith,

Rincon, and other places of the district. The addresses were made by Mrs. Etta Curtright, Rev. T.J. Goodall, Rev. N.W. White, and Prof. Archer, Dean of Morehouse College. All Officers were reelected. The meeting was a success spiritually, numerically, and financially. Mrs. E.R. Iiendersoa, President; Mrs. Clara Bennett, Treasurer, and Miss. Anna E. Maxwell, Recording Secretary (*Savannah Tribune* 2 Aug.1919, 6).

The Berean Baptist Association met in its 21ˢᵗ Annual Session at Central Baptist Church in Thunderbolt, GA, Rev. Wm. Gray, D.D., Moderator, opened the meeting. All old [current] officers were reelected. $2,900 was raised. The Women's Auxiliary of which Mrs. E.R. Henrison is president, and Mrs. Thurman [Thurmand], vice president, raised approximately $850.00. The report of the Association and the Women's Department showed a great improvement financially and numerically and the building of the school will soon be under way (*Savannah Tribune* 31 July1920, 1).

The Berean Association will convene next week at St. John Baptist Church, Rev. Wm. Gray, pastor. The sessions will start Tuesday morning and last throughout the week, ending Friday night. Rev. Wm. Gray, Moderator of the Association (*Savannah Tribune* 13 July1922, 1).

Achievements and Sessions:

The Berean Academy has opened her Theological Department for Ministers. Services were held at College Park. Rev. Priester preached the introductory sermon. Rev. N.H. Whitmer, in choice words presented him to the church (*Savannah Tribune* 30 Nov. 1922, 5).

The Berean Baptist Association is having a 5th Sunday meeting at Bethlehem Baptist Church, corner of Cuyler and Park Avenue, beginning Friday morning, December 29th and continue until Sunday (*Savannah Tribune* 29 Dec. 1922, 6).

The 44th Annual Session of the Berean Baptist District Sunday School and the thirty-second annual session of the Berean Baptist BTU will be held jointly at the Jerusalem Baptist Church, 45 Jefferson Street, on August 10-11. W. S. Roundfield, President Paul Brown (*Savannah Tribune* 3 Aug. 1944).

The Executive Board of the Berean Sunday School and BTU at a meeting held June 11, relative to the meeting of the convention scheduled to be held August 9-10 at Grace Baptist Church in Darian [Darien], decided to postpone said meeting until 1946. Instead, the coming meeting will be held at First Tabernacle Baptist Church on Alice Street in Savannah, GA (*Savannah Tribune* 28 Jan.1945, 1).

The Berean Association will meet at Second [African] Baptist Church, corner of President and Houston Streets on June 28-29 [1945]. The Association will give a great meeting at 3p.m. July 1, when Dr. L. L. Scott, Pastor, will speak from the subject "The Negroes Part in the New World Order." All churches in the Association will be present at that hour with their choirs (*Savannah Tribune* 21 June 1945, 3).

Moderator Rev. S. A. Baker of the Berean Baptist Association closed a very successful session at Second African Baptist Church, Sunday afternoon, with an address by Rev. L.L. Scott. The Association will meet next year at the Evergreen Baptist Church, Rev. E.A. Capers, Pastor (*Savannah Tribune* 5 July1945, 5). On Thursday, August 9th & 10th, the Berean District Sunday School and BTU will meet in joint session at the First Tabernacle Baptist Church with Dea. W.S. Roundfield, President of the Sunday School, and Dea. Paul Brown, President of the BTU (*Savannah Tribune* 2 Aug. 1945). The Berean Baptist Association will meet October 1st -3rd, At Nicholsonboro Baptist Church, Rev. S.A. Baker, Pastor. The Women will meet jointly with the parent body Wednesday morning, October 1st at 10 O'clock. October 2nd the Auxiliary will be held 10 a.m. at 1st Tabernacle Baptist Church, on Alice Street, Rev. H.W. Wilburn, Pastor. The

Young Peoples Dept. and Berean Minister's [Ministers']
Wives Auxiliary, Thursday. At 8p.m. Thursday night the
women will sponsor a Musical program with inspirational
messages. All Missions Societies, Young Girls' Circles and
Ministers Wives Auxiliaries are expected to report at this
session. Mrs. Inez Davis, President (*Savannah Tribune* 25
Sept. 1947,3). The Community 5th Sunday Union of the
Berean was held with Litway Baptist Church (*Savannah
Tribune* 4 Mar. 1948, 6). The Berean Baptist Association will
meet September 29th & 30th and October 1st at 1st Tabernacle
Baptist Church, Rev. H.W. Wilburn, Pastor, Rev. S.A. Baker,
Moderator (*Savannah Tribune* 23 Sept.1948, 2*)*.

Rev. Baker declines renomination. After serving as Moderator
of the Berean Baptist
Association for 4 years, the Rev. S.A. Baker declined
renomination during the annual meeting which convened
Wed.-Fri. at 1st Tabernacle Baptist Church. He expressed
his gratitude for the cooperation of the body during his
tenure and pledged his loyalty to the incoming Moderator.
The following officers were elected and installed: Rev. E.A.
Capers, Moderator; Rev. N.E. Holsey, Vice-Moderator;
Dea. N. Roberts, Recording Secretary; Rev. H.W. Wilburn,

Corresponding Secretary; Rev. J.C. McAllister, Missionary (*Savannah Tribune* 7 Oct. 1948*)*.

Rev. E.A. Capers, Pastor of 1st Evergreen Baptist Church was unanimously elected Moderator of the Berean Baptist Association which was in session at the 1st Tabernacle Baptist Church, Alice Street, last week. He succeeds Rev. S.A. Baker as Moderator *(Savannah Tribune* 7 Oct. 1948, 2).

The Savannah Tribune notes:

On Wednesday, October 27, at 5 p.m. at the home of Mrs. Inez Davis, the officers of the Berean Auxiliary were installed by Rev. E.A. Capers, Moderator of the Berean Baptist Association and Pastor of Evergreen Baptist Church. Preceding the services, the Board was called to order by the President, Mrs. Inez Davis, where business of vital importance was transacted. The Installation was held after which a tasty menu was served (*Savannah Tribune* 4 Nov. 1948, 3).

The Thunderbolt Community Union of the Berean Baptist Association met at Litway Baptist Church. A very informative session was held. The amount raised was $96.87. The next session will be held at the Wilmington Baptist Church. Rev. E.A. Capers, president, Mrs. Eloise Albright, reporter (*Savannah Tribune* 9 Feb.1950, 2).

The Berean Association brought to a close the most successful sessions of the Berean Baptist District Sunday School and Baptist Training Union. The sessions were held at First Friendship Baptist Church, Rev. G.R. Conner, pastor. Dea. S.C. White, Sr. was re-elected as president of the Sunday School and Dea. Paul Brown as president of the B.T.U. The convention will meet in August 1951 at Central Baptist Church, Rev. William Daniels, pastor (*Savannah Tribune* 17 Aug. 1950, 2).

Central Baptist Church, Rev. William Daniels, Pastor – The weekly services were attended with inspiration during the Berean Baptist Association that was held at First Friendship Baptist Church. Rev. William Daniels was re-elected Vice-Moderator of the Association (*Savannah Tribune* 12 July 1951, 2).

Sunday the District Meeting of the Berean Baptist Association was held at 1st Mt. Pleasant Baptist Church, Rev. Freddie Bonds, Pastor. Sunday will be Communion Day at Nicholsonboro Baptist Church, Rev. Thomas, Pastor (*Savannah Tribune* 3 Jan. 1952, 6).

The Women's Auxiliary to the Berean Baptist Association will meet July 9 – 12, at Happy Home Baptist Church, Rev. L.L. Small, Pastor. Officers of the Auxiliary: Mrs. M. Green,

President; Mrs. M. Ward, 1ˢᵗ Vice President; Mrs. M. Ward, 2ⁿᵈ Vice President; Mrs. V.G. Oliver, 3ʳᵈ Vice President; Mrs. Lizzie Cox(deceased) Treasurer; Mrs. R.B. Voss, Chairman of the Board; Mrs. E.H. Perry, Recording Secretary; and Mrs. A.L. Graves, Corresponding Secretary (*Savannah Tribune* 25 June 1953).

The Berean Annual School of Religious Education will open Monday, March 1ˢᵗ at 7:30 p.m. The classes will be held at 1ˢᵗ Evergreen Baptist Church, Bolton Street, East. Classes for instruction in all phases of Baptist Church activities will be offered. Rev. L.S. Stell, Supervisor of Instruction; Rev. E.P. Quarterman, Director (*Savannah Tribune* 18 Feb. 1954, 2).

"Berean Association to Meet Feb. 20," 1957 notes that the Berean Missionary Association will hold an Adjourned Session at First Evergreen Baptist Church, Rev. E.A. Capers, Pastor. An inspirational address was delivered by Juilus Brownlee, followed by introductory sermon by Rev. J. F. Mann. At the afternoon session, Peter Seabrooks gave an inspirational address, and the sermon was delivered by Rev. E. G. Lane. During the Women's Hour, Mrs. Marie G. Green presided. At the Laymen's Hour, C. Wimberly and J.H. Johnson presided. The Association concluded that night with a business meeting and sermon by Rev. R.L. Thomas (*Savannah Tribune* 9 Feb. 1957, 3).

Additional sessions:

Rev. E.A. Capers of the Berean Missionary Baptist Association announces that the Annual Session will meet with Emmanuel Baptist Church, Rev. J.C. McMillian is the pastor. The session will convene July 10-11. Theme: "The Cost of Discipleship" (*Savannah Tribune* 21 June 1958, 2).

Rev. Daniels and other members of Central Baptist Church will attend the 60th session of the Berean Association at Elm Grove Baptist Church, Meridian, GA (*Savannah Tribune* 11 July1959, 2).

The Berean District Union meeting was held at the Wilmington Baptist Church, Thunderbolt, on November 27, 28, &29. Rev. E.A. Capers, pastor. The sermon was delivered by Rev. R.E. Scott of Litway Baptist Church, Thunderbolt. The afternoon sermon was delivered by Rev. Willie Gwyn, pastor of College Park Baptist Church. James Butler, president (*Savannah Tribune* 5 Dec. 1959, 2).

The Annual Adjourned Session of the Berean Missionary Baptist Association will meet at 1st Evergreen Baptist Church, Wednesday, January 29, 1960. Officers: Rev. William Daniels, Moderator; Rev. L.S. Stell, Vice Moderator; Rev. L.S. Stell,

Jr., Secretary; Rev. L.L. Small Treasurer; and Rev. E.P. Quarterman, Corresponding Secretary (*Savannah Tribune* 5 Dec. 1959, 2).

"Berean Association to meet at Evergreen" expressed in article that the Annual Adjourned Session met at First Evergreen Baptist Church, Wednesday, January 29, 1960. The officers of the Association were Rev. E. A. Capers, Moderator; Rev. William Daniels, Vice Moderator; Rev. L. S. Stell, Jr., Secretary; Rev. L.L. Small, Treasurer; Rev. E.P. Quarterman, Corresponding Secretary (*Savannah Tribune*, 5 Dec.1959, 2).

The *Savannah Tribune* continues with a session's description. It writes that the 1st Evergreen Baptist Church, 622 E. Bolton Street, Rev. E.A. Capers, pastor, will host the Adjourned Session of the Berean Baptist Association, Wednesday, Jan. 27th. Rev. E.A. Capers, Moderator; Rev. L.S. Stell, Vice Moderator; and Rev. L.L. Small, Treasurer (23 Jan.1960).

CHAPTER IV

THE BEREAN ASSOCIATION 1961-1999

The 73rd Session of the Berean Missionary Baptist Association and the 52nd Sessions of the Women's Auxiliary of the Berean Association were hosted by Bethlehem Baptist Church, Savannah, GA, Rev. L. Scott Stell, Jr., Pastor, October 4, 5, 6, 1972 ("The 73rd Session of the Berean Missionary Baptist Association . . .). According to the Program Booklet, the officers were Rev. E. Aiken Capers, Moderator; Rev. William Daniels, Vice Moderator; Rev. L. Scott Stell, Jr., Clerk; Rev. Raymond L. Byrd, Treasurer; Rev. J. F. Mann, Statistician; Dea. S. L. White, Sr., President of Congress; Dea. John S. Delaware, President of Laymen's Department; Rev. E. Perry Quarterman, Institute Leader; Rev. William Franklin Stokes, II, Corresponding Secretary.

The Women's Auxiliary Officers, as noted in the program booklet were Mrs. Sarah White, President; Mrs. Nettie Merritt, Vice President at Large; Mrs. Lula L. Allen, Chairman Emeritus;

Mrs. Susie Dixon, Vice President; Mrs. Elizabeth Bolden, Mrs. Lucy Henderson, Mrs. Viola T. Robinson, Secretary of Board; Mrs. Marie Milton, Historian; Mrs. Catherine Smith, Mrs. Lillian Wilson, Music; Mrs. Fannie Woods, Treasurer; Mrs. Maggie Canty, Mrs. Lillian Wilson, Auditors; Mrs. L. S. Stell, Jr., Parliamentarian; Mrs. Henrietta Green, Mrs. Lillis Austin, Ways & Means; Mrs. Lillie T. Lewis, Recording Secretary ("The 73rd Session of the Berean Missionary Baptist Association . . .).

The theme for the session was "The Bible in Our Changing World," Isaiah 40:8, Association song, "Jesus the Light of the World" ("The 73rd Session of the Berean Missionary Baptist Association . . .).

The program participants included Rev. E. P. Quarterman who conducted the Study Period. Sis. Nettie Merritt was responsible for the Sunday School lesson. The Memorial Sermon was delivered by Rev. A. B. Brown; Rev. Joseph Smith was alternate for the Memorial Sermon. Mrs. Alfreida Shaw, from First African Baptist Church, responded to Bethlehem's welcome. Rev. J. F. Mann gave the introductory sermon, and Rev. William Daniels was the alternate. Sis. Lillie T. Lewis gave the inspirational address, and Mrs. Rosa B. Johnson was in charge of the Worship Committee. Echoes were reported from the National and State Conventions and from the WMU, City-Wide Week of Study. Sis. Rosa D. Johnson conducted the Youth Program; Miss Sharon Roundtree, Advisor, President.

Rev. Willie Gwyn presented the educational sermon, and Rev. R. E. Black was the alternate. Sis. S. M. Norris conducted the BTU [Baptist Training Union] Lesson. Rev. M. S. Brown gave the doctrinal sermon; the alternate was Rev. E. D. Smith. Mrs. Henrietta Green gave the response to the speech of the Women's Auxiliary President, Mrs. Sarah S. White. Moderator E. Aiken Capers gave his address, followed by an election ("The 73rd Session of the Berean Missionary Baptist Association . . .).

Reports were made by the following members: Mrs. William Daniels, Ministers' Wives; Mrs. Florence Gadson, Deacons' Wives; Mrs. T. Porter, Mrs. J. Vines, Badges; Mrs. B. Rivers, Mrs. I. Underwood, Personal Enrollment; Mrs. Sarah Williams, Child Welfare; Mrs. Collins, Citizenship; Mrs. Raine King, Mrs. M. Wiggins, Home and Family Life; Mrs. F. B. Scriven, Business and Professional Women; Mrs. Henrietta Green, Mrs. Lillie Austin, Ways & Means; Mrs. F. Wimberly, Foreign Mission; Mrs. Lillian Wilson, Music; Mrs. N. T. Jones, Home Mission; Mrs. M. L. Green, Mrs. V.T. Robinson, Mrs. I. C. Green, Letters; Dea. J. S. Delaware, Laymen; Dr. William Franklin Stokes, II gave the Missionary Sermon; Rev. James Stokes was the alternate ("The 73rd Session of the Berean Missionary Baptist Association . . .).

CHAPTER V

THE BEREAN ASSOCIATION
2000 -2023

A. Moderator Matthew Southall Brown, Sr.

The *Savannah Herald* reports the Berean Missionary Baptist Association was in session at First African Baptist Church, Rev. Thurmond N. Tillman, Pastor, beginning October 11, 2000. The 101st Annual Session was dedicated to the memory of Rev. Dr. William Daniels who served as Moderator of the Berean Association for over twenty years. This session included the voting of a Moderator, a Vice Moderator and other officers. The election was held Friday, October 13, 2000. Churches were to have youth at the Youth Hour, Thursday, October 12, 2000. Special greetings were made by New Era Missionary State Convention, the General Missionary Baptist State Convention, and other associations. Mrs. Jennifer Bailey from the Savannah Job Corp Center addressed the Association, topic, "Dealing with Job Issues." The following Pastors delivered sermons:

Rev. Frederick Fearbry, Thankful Baptist Church; Rev. Edward L. Ellis, Jr., Historic First Bryan Baptist Church; Rev. Keith Buckner, newly installed Pastor of Jerusalem Baptist Church, and Rev. Matthew Southall Brown, Sr., St. John Baptist Church. Noted officers: Rev. Matthew Southall Brown, Sr., Moderator; Rev. L. James Stell, Clerk; Rev. Willie Gwyn, Treasurer; Sis. Thomasina White, Corresponding Secretary; and Sis. Florrie B. Scriven, President of the Women's Auxiliary ("The Berean Missionary Association Now in Session").

Moderator Brown, Sr. continued to serve through the 112th Annual Session. His staff, 2008: Rev. Frederick A. Fearbry, 1st Vice Moderator; Rev. Larry J. Stell, 2nd Vice-Moderator; Rev. Michael S. Stamps, Clerk-P.B.; Rev. Wilson Scott, Jr., Treasurer-P.B.; Rev. Louis S. Stell, III, Statistician-P.B.; Sis. Mary G. Tootle, General Secretary, P.B.; Sis. Lillian Ellis, Reporter; Sis. Florrie B. Scriven, President-Women's Auxiliary; Sis. Linda Davis, 1st Vice President, Women's Auxiliary; Sis. Mildred Thomas, 2nd Vice President, Women's Auxiliary, Sis. Thomasina White, Recording Secretary, Women's Auxiliary; Sis. Janie B. Bowers, Treasurer, Women's Auxiliary; Sis. Lillian Spencer, Financial Secretary, Women's Auxiliary; Sis. Betty J. West, Dean of Congress; Dea. Robert Everson, President, Berean Congress; Rev. Edward Ellis, Bible Teacher; Dea. John [Johnnie] Paul Jones, Historian (Letter of Appreciation).

At the Berean Association Spring Break Program, 2008, 175 young people participated. The event was held at St. John, "The Mighty Fortress, Rev. George P. Lee, III, Pastor (Letter of Appreciation).

The Savannah Tribune continues to describe the activities of the Bereans:

> The 39th Annual Session of the Berean Congress will convene August 6,7, & 8, 2008 at Christ's Community Church at Morningside, 1805 E. Gwinnett Street, Pastor Kenneth Grant. The theme is "The Heavenly Vision – The Morals of the Church". The COPP [Certificate of Progress Program] classes are Effective Bible Reading, History of Baptist Doctrine and Survey of John (*Savannah Tribune* 30 Jul. 2008).
>
> The Berean Missionary Baptist Association of Georgia, Inc. along with the Clergymen in Action will co-host their first evangelistic Workshop May 8 -9, at First African Baptist Church of East Savannah, Rev. Thomas E. Williams, Pastor. Overall Theme for the workshop is ["Fishing on the Savannah Coast"] fishing on the Savannah Coast, the sub-theme is "An Evangelistic Thrust" (*Savannah Tribune* 29 Apr. 2009).
>
> 109th Annual Session, October 14-16, 2009, "The Heavenly Vision: The Mission of the Church," Second Arnold Baptist Church,

Savannah, GA, Rev. Richard Hall, Sr., Pastor; **Parent Body Officers:** Pastor, Rev. Matthew Southall Brown, Sr., Moderator; Rev. Dr. Frederick A. Fearbry, 1st Vice Moderator; Rev. Larry J. Stell, 2nd Vice Moderator; Rev. Michael S. Stamps, Sr., Clerk; Dr. Wilson Scott, Jr., Treasurer; Rev. Louis Stell, II, Statistician; Rev, Edward L. Ellis, Jr., Institute Leader; **Congress of Christian Education:** Dea. Robert Everson, President; Rev. Timothy Sheppard, 1st Vice President; Rev. Matthew Southall Brown, Jr., 2nd Vice President; Sis. Betty J. West, Dean; Dea. Robert Lee West, Statistician; **Women's Auxiliary:** Sis. Florrie B. Scriven, President; Sis. Annette Warren, 1st Vice President; Sis. Thomasina C. White, Recording Secretary; Sis. Josie M. Mattis, Corresponding Secretary; Sis. Lillian Spencer, Financial Secretary; Sis. Janie B. Bowers, Treasurer (Berean Missionary Baptist Association, Inc 109th Annual Session).

The Berean Congress of Christian Education is described by the *Savannah Tribune*:

> The 40th Annual Session of the Berean Congress of Christian Education will convene August 2,5, & 7, 2009 (SSPB-COPP). Theme: "Heavenly Vision: The Mission of the Church". Spiritual Reading: Ephesians 5:16-21; Acts 1:1-4. Host Church St. John Baptist Church, Rev. George P. Lee, III, pastor. COPP [Certificate of Progress Program] Classes are How the Bible Came to Be, Organizing the

Church for Christian Education, Church and Society, and others. Auxiliary to the Berean Missionary Association are: Rev. Matthew Southall Brown, Sr., Moderator; Sis. Florrie Screven, President of the Women's Auxiliary; Dea. Robert Everson, President of the Berean Congress; and Sis. Betty Jean West, Director/Dean (*Savannah Tribune* 22 Jul. 2009).

The 111th Annual Session, October 12 – 14, 2011 was held at Central Missionary Baptist Church, (Old Fort/Historic District), Savannah, GA, Rev. Larry J. Stell, Pastor. At this session, Moderator Matthew Southall Brown, Sr. expressed gratitude on behalf of the Association to Sis. Florrie Scriven and the Women's Auxiliary, Sis. Betty West, President Robert Everson and all planners of the Congress of Christian Education for a job well done and announced that he would not seek re-election as Moderator. The theme for this Session was "Solidarity with the Savior" Through Service and Sacrifice ("The Berean Missionary Baptist Association, Inc. 111th Annual Session").

Parent Body Officers included: Rev. Matthew Southall Brown, Sr., Moderator; Rev. Larry J. Stell, 2nd Vice Moderator; Rev. Michael S. Stamps, Sr., Clerk; Dr. Wilson Scott, Jr., Treasurer; Rev. Louis Stell, II, Statistician. The Congress of Christian Education included: Deacon Robert Everson, President; Rev. Timothy Sheppard, 1st Vice

President; Rev. Matthew Southall Brown, Jr., 2nd Vice President; Sis. Betty J. West, Dean; Dea. Robert Lee West, Statistician. The 42nd Session of the Congress of Christian Education was held **August** 1-5, 2011, theme: "Solidarity with the Savior through His Word"; Dea, Robert L. Everson, President; Sis. Betty Jean West, Director/Dean; Dr. Ann Marie James, Acting Dean ("The Berean Missionary Baptist Association, Inc. 111th Annual Session").

The Women's Auxiliary Officers included: Sis. Florrie B. Scriven, President; Sis. Annette M. Warren, 1st Vice President; Sis. Thomasina C. White, Recording Secretary; Sis. Josie M. Mattis, Corresponding Secretary; Sis. Lillian Spencer, Financial Secretary; and Sis. Janie B. Bowers, Treasurer ("The Berean Missionary Baptist Association, Inc. 111th Annual Session").

President Florrie Scriven writes that under her tenure the following events were initiated: the annual Sis. Elizabeth Bolden Agape Breakfast, a city-wide program for Savannah youth during their Spring Break, participation in the National Youth Day of Prayer, and the National Women's Day of Prayer. In addition, there were two international campaigns to help people of Tapio, Haiti with monetary contributions, medical supplies, and other human resources. This support was contributed annually to the National Baptist Convention, USA, Inc. Foreign Mission Board whose outreach included countries on the continent of Africa (Scriven 14 Mar. 2023).

Sis. Scriven also reported that at the 11th Elizabeth Bolden Agape Breakfast, April 26, 2011 at Bethlehem Missionary Baptist Church, Rev. Dr. Wilson Scott, Pastor, "seventeen teenagers," women over 80 years old, were honored: Sis. Ruth Wright, Abyssinia Missionary Baptist Church; Sis. Mildred Hicks, Bethlehem Missionary Baptist Church; Sis. Lillian Spencer, Central Missionary Baptist Church (Hitch Village); Sis. Arabelle Graham, First Bryan Missionary Baptist Church; Sis. Thelma Washington, First Bryan Missionary Baptist Church; Sis. Rachel Brown, First Friendship Missionary Baptist Church; Sis. Gertrude Prince, First Union Missionary Baptist Church; Sis. Gertrude Mitchell, Happy Home Missionary Baptist Church; Sis. Gloria Wright, Litway Missionary Baptist Church; Sis. Elizabeth Bolden, Second Arnold Missionary Baptist Church; Sis. Edna Dingle, Second Arnold Missionary Baptist Church; Sis. Francis McLaurin, Tremont Temple Missionary Baptist Church; Sis. Wilmotine Gwyn, Zion Hill Missionary Baptist Church; Sis. Mary Matthews, First Jerusalem Missionary Baptist Church; Min. Beatrice Lewis, St John Missionary Baptist Church (Mighty Fortress); Sis. Josephine Jackson, Macedonia Missionary Baptist Church; Sis. Margaret Bailey, Happy Home Missionary Baptist Church (Scriven Apr. 2023).

The Women's Auxiliary Queens Program was held. Deaconess Janie B. Bowers was Coordinator and Deaconess Evelyn

Green was Co-Coordinator. The reigning Queen, 2010 – 2011, was Deaconess Shirley Chester, Bolton Street Baptist Church, Rev. Perry Tyson, Pastor. The contestants were Sis. Annie Brown, 1st Union Baptist Church, Sis. JoAnn Wilson, 2nd St. John Baptist Church, and Sis. Josephine Green, 1st Friendship Baptist Church ("The Berean Missionary Baptist Association, Inc. 111th Annual Session").

At the Women's Auxiliary Hour, Sis. Evelyn Green served as Second Vice President and presided during the hour. Noted participants were Sis. Almethia Frazier, Deaconess Rosa Lee Brisbane, Rev. Paul Sheppard, Evangelist Thelma Jenkins, Sis. Wilmotine Gwyn, Sis. Diane Wagner, Sis. Gertrude Prince, Sis. Edna Artis, Sis. Rachel Brown, Sis. Naomi Thomas, Sis. Mary Coleman, Sis. Alberta Milton, Sis. Cynthia White. At the Women's Auxiliary President's Hour. Sis. Annette M. Warren served as First Vice President and presided during this hour. Noted participants were Dea. Eddie Sampson, Rev. Elizabeth Lucky, Rev. Robert Bolden, Sis. Carolyn George, Rev. Dr. Sinclair Thorne (President of Foreign Mission Board), Rev. Guy Malcolm Hodge III, Bro. Zachariah Patterson, Rev. Larry Stell, Rev. Paul Little, Sis. Carrie Rouse, Sis. Shirley Wright, Moderator Matthew Southall Brown, Sr., and President's Address by Sis. Florrie B. Scriven ("The Berean Missionary Baptist Association, Inc. 111th Annual Session").

Women's Auxiliary Standing Committees: **Berean Queen Contest** – Sis. Janie B. Bowers, Sis. Evelyn Green, Sis. Diana Stamps, Sis. Carolyn Scott; Young **People's Department** – Rev. Phelecia Barnes, Interim Youth Director, Sis. Wanda Chaplin, Sis. Joan Green, Sis. Gwen Arnold, Sis. Claudena Dudley, Sis. Diane Poole; **Deacon Wives, Widows, and Deaconesses** – Sis. Mary T. Roberson, Sis. Evelyn Green, Sis. Betty Ellison; **Foreign Mission** – Sis. Carolyn Scott-Toure, Sis. Theresa Baker, Sis. Florrie Scriven; **Personal Enrollment** – Sis. Frances McLaurin, Sis. Evelyn Green, Sis. Alberta Milton, Sis. Carolyn Scott; **Registration** – Sis. Teresa Van-Baker, Sis. Annett Warren; **Prayer Warriors** – Sis. Wilmotine Gwyn, Sis. Diane Wagner, Sis. Arabell Graham; **Ministers' Wives and Widows** – Sis. Lottie Brown, Sis. Wilmotine Gwyn, Sis. Diane Stamps; **Home Mission** – Sis. Josephine F. Sanders, Sis. Carolyn Scott-Toure, Rev. Mary Johnson, Sis. Ruth Wright; **Historical Search** – Sis. Lillian Spencer; **Ushers** – Sis. Shirley Miller, Sis. Claudena Dudley, Sis. Josephine F. Sanders, Sis. Julia Johnson; **Musician** – Sis. Kathy Morgan; Appointed Committees: **Budget Committee**- Sis. Lillian Spencer, Sis. Janie Bowers, Sis. Annette Warren, Sis. Thomasina White; **Baptist Women Day of Prayer** – Rev. Elizabeth Lucky, Min. Beatrice Lewis, Rev. Mary Johnson, Evangelist Thelma Jenkins ("The Berean Missionary Baptist Association, Inc. 111th Annual Session").

The 112th Annual Session, October 16-19, 2012, Greater Friendship Baptist Church, Savannah, GA, Rev. Nathaniel Small, Jr.; **Parent Body Officers:** Pastor, Rev. Matthew Southall Brown, Sr., Moderator; Rev. Larry J. Stell, 2nd Moderator; Rev. Wilson Scott, Jr., Treasurer; Rev. Michael S. Stamps, Sr., Clerk; **Congress of Christian Education Officers:** Dea. Robert Everson, President; Rev. Timothy M. Sheppard, 1st Vice President; Rev. Matthew Southhall Brown, Jr., 2nd Vice President; Sis. Betty J. West, Director-Dean; **Women's Auxiliary Officers:** Sis. Florrie B. Scriven, President; Sis. Annette M. Warren, 1st Vice President; Sis. Thomasina C. White, Recording Secretary; Sis. Josie M. Mattis, Corresponding Secretary; Sis. Lillian Spencer, Financial Secretary; Sis. Janie Bowers, Treasurer (Brown).

The Election Process

The election process was agreed to by the body. **Eligibility,** in order to be considered eligible, a member church must have registered at the last two (2) consecutive Annual Sessions. In this case, years were 2011-2012. Eligibility was determined from the registration records. **Voting Delegates,** in order to make the election process as fair as possible, each member church was allowed five (5) delegate votes upon establishing eligibility. These five (5) delegates had to be registered at the session when the vote was taking place. **Voting,** the method of voting was by ballot. **Oversight** and integrity of the election was of utmost concern, so an election committee was established to oversee the balloting and outcome of the election ("Election").

B. Moderator Clarence "Teddy" Williams, Jr.

The official ballot for Moderator included candidates: Pastor Larry J. Stell and Pastor Clarence Williams. With Moderator Matthew Southall Brown, Sr., stepping down as Moderator, the election secured Rev. Clarence "Teddy" Williams as the new Moderator at the 112th Annual Session.

Rev. Dr. Clarence Williams, Jr., Pastor of Pilgrim Baptist Church of Savannah was elected Moderator. His goal was to achieve structure, accountability, and tenure. His vision was one of "Greater Works."

According to the Program, "Installation Service for Rev. Dr. Clarence Williams, Jr., Moderator-Elect," Moderator Williams's installation was Saturday, January 5, 2013, 12 Noon, at First Tabernacle Missionary Baptist Church, Savannah, GA. Rev. Dr. E.L. Hart, Moderator Zion Missionary Baptist Association, presided, and Rev. Dr. Walter Glover, Moderator Union Missionary Baptist Association (Macon, GA) was the Proclaimer of the Word. Installation Committee: Rev. Marque C. Johnson, Chairman; Rev. Timothy Sheppard, Co-Chair; Rev. Matthew S. Brown, Jr., Co-Chair; Rev. Guy Hodge, III, Rev. Q. Morris, Rev. Gregory Tyson, Rev. Ronald

Gregory, Rev. Keith T. Bruen, Deacon R. Stephens (Happy Home); Deacon Bryant (Tremont Temple); Sister Kathy Morgan, Deacon McArthur Holmes (1st Tabernacle); Sister Gloria Richardson (Happy Home); Sister Angela Page (1st Tabernacle); Sister Lawanda Tillman (1st African); Sister Vanessa A. Young (1st Friendship); Sister Annette Mitchell (Tremont Temple); Sister Lula Polite (1st Nazareth); Sister B.Y. Mack (Connor's Temple); Sister Catherine Jackson (New Zion); Deacon Florida Hunt (Bethel Baptist); Sister Lula Baker (Thankful Baptist); Sister Joan Green (2nd Arnold); Sister Shavondra Caeser (1st Union); First Tabernacle Missionary Baptist Church Culinary Committee (J. Abney, Coordinator); Sister Wilmotine Gwyn and Sister Janie Bowers (Honorary Members) (Program, "Installation Service for Rev. Dr. Clarence Williams, Jr., Moderator-Elect").

The 112th Adjourned Session was held at Thankful Missionary Baptist Church, Savannah, GA, Rev. Paul Sheppard, Pastor, Rev. Dr. Clarence Williams, Jr., Moderator ("The Berean Missionary Baptist Association, Inc. 112th Adjourned Session"). The Program, "Installation Service for Rev. Dr. Clarence Williams, Jr., Moderator-Elect" states the Session began Wednesday, January 23, 2013, Purpose Driven Churches, "Building on a legacy of great association leaders."

Moderator Matthew Southall Brown, Sr. presented the gavel to the new Moderator, Rev. Dr. Clarence Williams, Jr. Rev. Joseph Hoze presented the Introductory Sermon. At the Women's Auxiliary,

Sis. Florrie B. Scriven presiding, Praise and Worship was conducted by Sis. Betty Ellison. The welcome was presented by Sis. Mary Reid, Thankful Missionary Baptist Church, and the response was done by Sis. Jo Ann Wilson. Other members on the Program included Rev. Belinda Harrington, Consecration Prayer; Evangelist Thelma Jenkins, Reflections of Deceased Members; Sis. Diana Stamps, Introduction of Guest Speaker; Sis. Yvonne Pryor, Interim Director of Inner-City Mission and Baptist Center Sojourner of Savannah, Inc.; Sis. Alberta Milton and Sis. Lillie Evans, Offering. At the Youth Hour, Rev. Barbara Simmons served as Interim Young People's Director, and remarks were made by Sis. Evelyn Green ("The Berean Missionary Baptist Association, Inc. 112th Adjourned Session").

Officers at the 112th Adjourned Session according to the Program Booklet: **Parent Body**, Rev. Dr. Clarence Williams, Jr., Moderator; Rev. Larry J. Stell, 2nd Vice Moderator; Rev. Dr. Wilson Scott, Jr., Treasurer; Rev. Michael S. Stamps, Sr., Clerk; Rev. Louis Stell, III, Statistician, and Rev. Matthew Southall Brown, Sr., Moderator Emeritus, 25 plus years of leadership. **Congress of Christian Education**, Dea. Robert Everson, President; Rev. Timothy Sheppard, 1st Vice President; Rev. Matthew Southall Brown, Jr., 2nd Vice President; Sis. Betty West, Dean; Dea. Robert L. West, Statistician. **Women's Auxiliary**, Sis. Florrie B. Scriven, President; Sis. Annette M. Warren, 1st Vice President; Sis. Evelyn Green, 2nd

Vice President; Sis. Thomasina C. White, Recording Secretary; Sis. Angelyne Johnson, Asst. Recording Secretary; Sis. Lillian Spencer, Financial Secretary; Sis. Janie Bowers, Treasurer; Rev. Barbara Simmons, Interim Youth Director ("The Berean Missionary Baptist Association, Inc. 112th Adjourned Session").

The 113th Berean Missionary Baptist Association, Inc. met October 17-19, 2013, at Second African Baptist Church, Savannah, GA, Rev. C. MeGill Brown, Pastor with Moderator Rev. Dr. Clarence Williams, Jr. His focus was structure, accountability, and tenure. His thrust was Developing Purpose Driven Churches for the 21st Century, according to the Berean Association Executive Board Meeting August 31, 2013, planning session for 113th.

The 113th Parent Body Opening Session and Registration were Friday, October 18, 2013, 9:00 a.m. The Bible Institute, Acts 17:11, was conducted by Pastor C. MeGill Brown. The Association Sermon given by Rev. Guy M. Hodge, III, Rev. Paul Sheppard, the alternate. There were plans for church enrichment seminars: Ministers, Rev. P. Sheppard, and Rev. Q. Morris, Coordinators; Finance and Trustees, Sis. S. Cutter and Dea. Bernard Conyers, Coordinators; Ushers/Greeters and Nurses, Sis. A. Sills and Sis. Julia Johnson, Coordinators; Choir/Music, Evangelist Jameson, Bro. Johnny Perkins, and Rev. Marque Johnson, Coordinators; General Church Leadership, Sis. Cynthia Fearbry and Sis. Mary Page,

Coordinators; culminating the Evangelistic Crusade, the Evangelistic Sermon was by Rev. A. Piper, followed by Baptism. The Saturday morning, plans were made for Bible Institute, Acts 17:11, by Pastor C. MeGill Brown. At the business meeting, Moderator Clarence Williams proposed constitutional amendments to include divisions, officers, election process, appointed positions. Youth Breakout Sessions were coordinated by Rev. Paul Little, Sis. Angela Page, Sis. Gwen Sheppard, Rev. Ricardo Manuel, and Rev. Barbara Simmons. Sis. Florrie B. Scriven, President, oversaw the Women's Auxiliary Hour with Sis. A. Warren, 1st Vice President of Women, presiding. Rev. Dr. Richard Hall, 2nd Vice Moderator, presided during Moderator Williams Annual Address Hour.

The Program Booklet states the 113th Adjourned Session of the Berean Missionary Association, Inc. was held January 25, 2014, hosted by Central Baptist Church, Savannah, GA, Rev. Larry J. Stell, Pastor, Rev. Dr. Clarence Williams, Jr. Moderator. The theme or mantra was "Developing Purpose Driven Churches for 21st Century Ministry."

Members were appointed to the following committees Time and Place 2014, Resolution 2014, Calendar 2014, Election Committee 2014, and others that were needed. The Business included Finance, Children and Youth, Laymen, Historian, and Auxiliaries 2013. Partnerships with Savannah Chatham YFA, Shaw University

Trustees and American Red Cross were discussed. The Introductory Sermon was by Rev. Paul Sheppard, Pastor, Thankful Baptist Church, Savannah, Ga.

The youth were engaged in spiritual and social enrichment and in preparing for their Youth Hour. During the Women's Auxiliary Hour, Sis. Florrie B. Scriven presided. Program participants included: Sis. Betty Ellison, Praise and Worship Leader; Sis. Almetia Frazier, Welcome; Sis. Diana V. Stamps, Response to Welcome; Rev. Lolita Hickman, Pastor, Trinity Baptist Church, Consecration Prayer; Evangelist Thelma Jenkins, Deceased Members Reflection; Sis. Evelyn Green, Introduction of Guest Speaker; Sis. Ella Williamson, Presenter, Director of St. Joseph/Candler Afro-American Center, Savannah, Georgia; Sis. Betty West, Presentation of Appreciation; and Sis. Denise Prince and Sis. Theresa Van Baker, Finance. **The Officers of the Parent Body**: Moderator, Dr. Clarence Williams, Jr; 1st Vice Moderator, Rev. Larry J. Stell; 2nd Vice Moderator, Rev. Richard Hall; Treasurer, Rev. Joseph Hoze; Clerk, Rev. Michael S. Stamps, Sr., Statistician, Rev. Louis Stell, II, and Moderator Emeritus, Rev. Matthew Southall Brown, Sr. **The Officers of Congress of Christian Education:** President, Rev. Timothy Sheppard; Vice President, Rev. Matthew Southall Brown, Jr., Dean, Sis. Betty J. West; General Director, Dea. McArthur Holmes. **Women's Auxiliary Officers:** President, Sis. Florrie B. Scriven; 1st Vice President, Sis. Annette M.

Warren; 2nd Vice President, Sis. Evelyn Green; Recording Secretary, Sis. Thomasina White. **The Appointed Finance Committee:** Rev Joseph Hoze, Parent Body; Rev. Nathaniel Small, Jr., Parent Body; Sis. Dorothy Bouligny, Congress; Dea. Willie Brown, S. E. White Scholarship; Sis. Denise Prince, Women's Auxiliary.

More information located in Savannah Tribune expresses the following:

The Berean Missionary Baptist Association 113th Adjourned Session will convene on Saturday, January 25, 2014, at Central Baptist Church 738 Hitch Drive, Savannah, GA, Rev. Clarence "Teddy" Williams, Moderator; Rev. Larry Stell, Host Pastor. The Berean Association Congress of Christian Education annual session, 45th Annual Session, will host their monthly planning meeting at Central Baptist Church in Thunderbolt, GA (*Savannah Tribune* 113th Adjourned Session).

The 115th Annual Session was held at First Union Baptist Church, Rev. Matthew S. Brown, Jr., Pastor. Rev. Dr. Clarence Williams, Jr., Moderator, firmly supported his goal of structure, accountability and tenure and his mantra of "Developing Purpose Driven Churches for 21st Century." He affirmed that his vision statement was "The Berean Missionary Baptist Association, Inc. will be an association noted for spiritual excellence by ensuring that member churches reach their God-given potential to exalt the Savior, evangelize the lost and equip the Saints" ("The Berean Missionary Baptist Association, Inc. 115th Annual Session.")

At the 115th Annual Session, Sis. Evelyn Green became the President of the Women's Auxiliary of the Berean Missionary Baptist Association, Inc. in 2015.

According to the Minutes of Sis. Carolyn Scott, the matters of Business included Rev. Richard Hall, Sr. opening floor for nominees for Moderator; there were no other nominees than Rev. Clarence Williams. Moderator Clarence Williams was introduced by Rev. Andre Osborne, pastor of First Tabernacle Baptist Church. On Saturday, "Greater Works" 2016 indicated that the election of Moderator was held from 9:00 a.m. – 2:00 p.m. for voting delegates only. Youth Enrichment Sessions were held at Connor's Temple Baptist Church conducted by Rev. Andre Osborne, Rev. Matthew S. Brown, Sr., and Dr. Patricia Harris.

Moderator Clarence "Teddy" Williams, 116th Annual Session, 2016, "Greater Works," Purpose Driven Churches of the Berean Missionary Baptist Association, Inc. According to the "Greater Works" booklet, 2016, the Mission of the Berean Missionary Baptist Association, Inc. is to provide fellowship, training, and sharing of resources with member churches to advance the work of the Lord, adopted January 2013. Moderator Williams thanked the Executive Board, Pastors, and supporters for working with him for the past four years. Due to the upcoming elections, Moderator Williams remarked in booklet "Greater Works" 2016 We have more than 15,000 plus members in our association, and we can be a VOICE in this year's election on all ballot items."

The church enrichment seminars were presented: Clergy, "What the Bible Says to Ministers," and "Conflict Resolution," held at Thankful Baptist Church and taught by Rev. Damion Gordon and Rev. Bobby Berryman; Youth Directors, "Are We Speaking Their Language?" held at Thankful Baptist Church and taught by Rev. Terrence Pinckney; and Church Music, "Is Music Edifying or Entertaining?" held at Connor's Temple Baptist Church and taught by Mr. J. Perkins and Rev. W. Rice ("Greater Works" 2016).

116th Annual Session Officers: **Parent Body Officers**, Rev. Clarence Williams, Moderator; Rev. Richard Hall, Sr., 1st Vice Moderator; Rev. Dr. C. MeGill Brown, 2nd Vice Moderator; Rev. Joseph Hoze, Treasurer; Sis. Carolyn Scott, Secretary; Rev. Michael S. Stamps, Sr., Clerk; Rev. Matthew Southall Brown, Sr., Moderator Emeritus; Women's **Auxiliary Officers**, Sis. Evelyn Green, President; Rev. Barbara Simmons, 1st Vice President; Sis. Pamela Swain, 2nd Vice President; **Congress of Christian Education Officers,** Rev. Timothy Sheppard, President; Dea. James Green, 1st Vice President; Sis. Kathy Morgan, Dean; **Laymen's Auxiliary Officers,** Bro. Julius

Green, President; Bro. Raleigh Stephens, Vice President; Bro. Cecil Gwyn, Secretary ("Greater Works" 2016).

Sis. Carolyn B. Scott emailed Minutes, 11-14-22, the Berean Missionary Baptist Association, Inc. 116th Annual Session, October 14, 2016 - October 16, 2016.

The Minutes included the Official Opening – Friday, October 14, 2016 – 9am, Moderator Clarence Williams, Jr., Presiding, Thankful Baptist Church. The Bible Institute was led by Rev. Willie Rice. New churches were welcomed: Mt. Hermon Baptist Church, True Love Baptist Church, and First Mt. Sinai Baptist Church. Rev. Thurman Tillman discussed voting and distributed form "I Am a Faithful Voter." Members were encouraged to vote early and to utilize absentee ballots. The Association Sermon, "Hold On," was delivered by Rev. Matthew Southall Brown, Jr. with Rev. Bernard Bryant as alternate to deliver Sermon, Friday, October 14. President Rev. Kenneth B. Martin of the General Missionary Baptist Convention of Ga, Inc. gave remarks on the state of the Convention. The Women's Session was opened by President Evelyn Green. At this session, Senator Regina Thomas discussed voting for the November election. At the Women's Hour, Minister Barbara Simmons presided. President Green was introduced by her sister, Sis. Naomi Reed ("Greater Works" 2016).

The Partners of the Berean Association: Chatham-Savannah Youth Futures Authority (YFA), Greenbriar Children's Center, Shaw University, American Red Cross, Queensborough National Bank, New Generation School of Theology, Savannah Regional Central Labor Council ("Greater Works" 2016).

Laymen's Auxiliary, Dea. Julius Green, President, at the 116th Annual Session, provided a forum of presenters: Terry L. Enoch, Savannah Chatham County Public School System (SCCPSS Chief of Campus Police), and Karen Hamilton, Unit Director (Frank Callen Boys and Girls Club) ("Greater Works" 2016).

"Greater Works" 2016 listed the following churches as member churches at the 116th Annual Session:

Abyssinia Missionary Baptist Church (Rev. Butler), Bethel Baptist Church (Rev. Baker), Bethlehem Baptist Church (Rev. Scott), Bolton Street Baptist Church (Rev. Tyson), Brampton Baptist Church, Brownsville Baptist Church; Bunn Memorial Baptist Church (Rev. Cutter), Central Baptist Church in the Old Fort (Rev. Stell), Central Missionary Baptist Church of Thunderbolt, GA (Rev. T. Sheppard), Christ Memorial Baptist Church (Rev. Broxton), Clifton Baptist Church (Rev. Pinckney), College Park Baptist Church (Rev. O'Berry-Elect), Connor's Temple Baptist Church (Rev. Burrell), First African Missionary Baptist Church of East Savannah

(Rev. T. Williams), First Ebenezer Baptist Church (Rev. Singleton), First Evergreen Missionary Baptist Church (Rev. Gregory), First Friendship Baptist Church (Rev. Chavis), First Metropolitan Baptist Church (Rev. McClendon), First Mt. Bethel Baptist Church (Rev. Smith), First Nazareth Missionary Baptist Church (Rev. Wilbourn), First Smyrna Baptist Church (Rev. Bennett), First Tabernacle Missionary Baptist Church (Rev. Osborne), First Union Missionary Baptist Church (Rev. Brown, Jr.), Greater Friendship Baptist Church, (Rev. C. Brown), Happy Home Baptist Church (Bishop McNeal), Historic First African Baptist Church (Rev. Tillman), Historic First Bryan Baptist Church (Rev. James), Historic Second African Baptist Church, Jonesville Baptist Church of the P.A.W. (Bishop Rodgers), Litway Baptist Church (Rev. Small), Macedonia Baptist Church (Rev. Rice), Mt. Hermon Baptist Church (Rev. Philips), Mt. Moriah Baptist Church (Rev. G. Hall), Mt. Olivet Baptist Church (Rev. A. Staley), Mt. Tabor Baptist Church (Rev. Blackshear), Mt. Zion Baptist Church (Rev. Stamps), New Generation Full Gospel Baptist (Bishop Darden), New Zion Baptist Church (Rev. Bryant), Pilgrim Baptist Church of Savannah (Rev. C. Williams), Richfield Baptist Church (Rev. Powers), Second Arnold Missionary Baptist Church (Rev. R. Hall), Second Ebenezer Baptist

Church (Rev. Manuel), Second St. John Missionary Baptist Church (Rev. Johnson), St. John Divine Baptist Church (Rev. Piper), St. John Missionary Baptist Church (Rev. Lee), Thankful Baptist Church (Rev. P. Sheppard), Tremont Temple Missionary Baptist Church (Rev. Morris), True Love Baptist Church (Rev. Watson), Trinity Baptist Church (Rev. Hickman), Zion Hill Baptist Church (Rev. Hoze) ("Greater Works" 2016).

The Minutes indicated the Adjourned Session, January 14, 2017, will be hosted by First Smyrna Baptist Church and, the Strategic Leadership will be discussed at the next Executive Board Meeting.

Rev. Joseph Hoze gave the financial report. The report included 18 churches registered, balance - $38,800.

Moderator Williams encouraged members to volunteer at the Red Cross. Forms were available to sign up. He thanked the Red Cross for all that they do. The representative was Sis. Esther Sheppard, Southeast and Coastal Georgia, Executive Director. Sis. Sheppard is the wife of Rev. Paul Sheppard, the Pastor of Thankful Baptist Church.

Rev. Carolyn Dowse, Senior Saints Coordinator, discussed various activities and training at Mt. Zion, Tuesday, and Thursday.

Holy Communion observance was delivered by Rev. T.N. Tillman, Saturday, at the closing of the 116th Annual Session.

At the 116th Adjourned Session, Moderator Clarence Williams, "Greater Works" 2017 booklet says the 116th Adjourned Session and Evangelism Emphasis of the Berean Missionary Baptist Association, Inc. notes the Association as "Purpose Driven Churches," the website as www.thebereanassociation.org and the address as 5032 Savannah, GA 31414.

At the Adjourned Session, the Children and Youth Ministry convened at Growing in Grace Church from 9:00 a.m. – 2:00 p.m. with inspirational and educational activities. Lunch was served at 12:00 p.m. at no cost ("Greater Works," 2017).

"Greater Works" 2017 listed the following guests for the 116th Adjourned Session: Rev. Dr. Roy Thomas, General Missionary Baptist Convention of Georgia, Inc. 8th District President, the Evangelistic Service Preacher; Sis. Lillian Baptiste, Women's Health, Women's Auxiliary Presenter; Rev. Carl Gilyard, State of Georgia, Laymen's Auxiliary Presenter; Pastor Ricky Temple, Long-term recovery after Hurricane Matthew, Parent Body Presenter; Sis. Ann Levette, Savannah Chatham County Public Schools, Children and Youth Presenter; Alderman Van Johnson, Citizenship, Children and Youth Presenter.

Officers/Positions not listed in "Greater Works," 2016 but listed in 2017 were Sis. Carolyn Dowse, Senior Citizens; Rev. Ricardo Manuel, Social/Civic; Dean Kathy Morgan, Christian Leadership

Schools; and Sis. Sandra Williams, Administrative Assistant to the Moderator.

The Minutes of The Berean Missionary Baptist Association, Inc. 116th Adjourned Session says the Association was held at Zion Hill Baptist Church, Rev. Joseph Hoze, Pastor, January 27-28, 2017. According to Secretary, Sis. Carolyn B. Scott, the Board meeting and registration were held January 27, 2017. The Evangelistic Service and Baptism were also held.

January 28, 2017, during devotion, the Bible Institute was conducted by Rev. C. MeGill Brown. The Association was called to order by Moderator Clarence Williams.

The following business was discussed:

- Communication from First African Baptist Church announcing a concert of old songs, February 12, 2017.
- Presentation from Ms. Vickie Beavers with a request for churches to organize a basketball league.
- Announcement from the *Savannah Herald* newspaper of its new location, 2135 Roland Avenue, Suite "B".
- Children's inclusion in church registration, "Growing in Grace."
- The contacting of inactive churches to determine membership status by the Reclamation Committee

members: Rev. Thurman Tillman, Chairman, Sister Mary Coleman, and Sis. Julia Johnson.

- The acceptance of the Strategic Planning Committee: Sister Stephanie Cutter, Rev. Carolyn Dowse, Rev. Andre Osborne, Minister Sandra Williams, Brother Edward Chisholm.

- The acceptance of the History Committee: Sis. Ivy Richardson, Rev. Charles L. Hoskins, Sis. Emma Jean Conyers, Sis. Verlene Lampley, Dea. Willie Brown, and Sis. Georgia Benton.

- Women's Auxiliary Report – Distributed

- Congress of Christian Education report, Rev. Timothy Sheppard – Rev. Marques Johnson, Sr. and congregation of Second St. John Baptist Church will host the next Congress. Members were encouraged to support leadership schools.

The Christian Leadership School Manual defines the Christian Leadership School:

> In July 1997, several Christian educators came together in Nashville, Tennessee, for the purpose of revising the SSPB's Christian education efforts to provide a comprehensive program of Christian education to reach, teach, and develop the masses

in a continuous, systematic manner. The goal was to develop a Christian Leadership School manual that would provide a comprehensive, user-friendly manual to serve the educational needs of the constituents of the National Baptist Convention, USA, Inc. The contents of the manual represented the total program for Christian education as proposed by the Division of Christian Education Accreditation and Credentials of the Sunday School Publishing Board, National Baptist Convention, USA, Inc. *(The Christian Leadership School Manual* 10).

The Christian Leadership School Manual defines the COPP as the Certificate of Progress Program, organized at the Sunday School Publishing Board in October 1937. The objectives of COPP:

(1) To increase the biblical knowledge of the student;

(2) To create an understanding of the Baptist faith;

(3) To provide an educational structure that will develop candidates qualified for teaching and leadership positions;

(4) To provide incentives for the candidates to complete the program; and

(5) To produce trained church leaders (*The Christian Leadership School Manual* 38).

Other business:

- Laymen's Auxiliary – Assisted Greenbriar Center with cleanup following Hurricane Matthew; adopted Frank Callen Boys and Girls Club as partners.

- Senior Saints – Distributed report. Volunteers are needed. Certificates of completion for the first class in Senior Saints Ministry Training Course distributed.

- Berean retreat, scheduled for May 19 and 20 at St. Simons Island.

- Members were encouraged to recruit age group 35-50 for Berean.

- Greenbriar Children's Center Report – Executive Director, Gena Taylor, thanked the Association for all the work and support to the center: chairs, tables, new flooring, fence, and security system in emergency shelter buildings. A volunteer team from Maine assisted with the work. The Laymen cleaned the grounds following the storm. Another project included the installation of lights in the gym to be completed by the middle of February. Director Taylor thanked everyone for volunteering with the Christmas gift wrapping project, held every December, [usually], at the Oglethorpe Mall, usually.

- Martin L King, Pharmacy – Mr. Kirankumar Patel, owner, asked for support of the association members and Moderator Williams asked pastors on the MLK Corridor to discuss prospects with the pharmacy. Mr. Patel donated $400 to the association for youth.

- Mr. Jerome Irwin, President of the Central Labor Council, made remarks and presented a resolution that was accepted by the Association.

Rev. Ricardo Manuel, 2016 host pastor, delivered the sermon title, "Tomorrow," Exodus 8:1.

Women Session – President Evelyn Green presided. President Emerita, Sis.

Florrie Scriven gave remarks and thanked women for support of the Foreign Mission. Total money reported to foreign mission was $3,000. Members were encouraged to attend the General Missionary Baptist Convention of GA, Inc., Association Presidents' meeting in Macon. Members were encouraged to attend so that the attendance trophy would remain in the First District. Sis. Stephanie Cutter introduced the speaker of the hour, Sis. Lillian Baptiste, whose topic was "Women's Health."

Additional Information:

(1) The Laymen Session – Dea. Julius Green, President, speaker, his topic was "Self-Examination."

(2) Rev. Ricky Temple gave remarks and discussed the aftermath of Hurricane Matthew.

He encouraged all to be hurricane strong, be prepared emotionally, physically, and individually.

(3) The Financial Summary was made by Rev. Joseph Hoze:

- Brought forward $33,000, expenses $30,310. Session registrations
- 24 churches
- 36 clergy
- 16 men
- 73 women
- Financial report was accepted and filed for audit.

The *Savannah Tribune* notes the following about the Berean Association:

Berean Association Women's Auxiliary will celebrate the 17th Elizabeth Bolden Agape Breakfast of Saturday, May 6, 2017, at 9:00 a.m. The Celebration will take place at 2nd St. John Missionary Baptist Church, Rev. Marques Johnson, pastor. A spiritual service will include prayers, songs, and a 'Wear a Crown' Hat Presentation. A delicious breakfast will be served. Rev. Clarence Williams, Moderator; Sis. Evelyn Green, President (*Savannah Tribune* 29 Mar. 2017).

Topics of interest as reported in Minutes, located in "Greater Works," 2017: (1) Moderator Williams welcomed new pastor of Greater Friendship Baptist Church. (2) Dr. Smith from South University discussed United Way and Doctoral Degrees in Ministry. (3) Means of working with school bus drivers and port drivers. (4) Rev. Thurman Tillman encouraged voting, distributing forms "I Am a Faithful Voter." (5) Dr. Nasir Ahmad presented information on inter-faith initiatives. (6) Rev. Kenneth B. Martin, State President, addressed the Association as a presidential candidate for the General Missionary Baptist Convention of GA, Inc. (GMBC) and discussed relief for Savannah in the aftermath of hurricane Matthew. (7) Bereans should contact Min. Carolyn Dowse or Pastor Scott of Bethlehem for information on free Homiletic Class. (8) Remarks were made by Rev. Joseph Hoze, President of Interdenominational Association.

Also, in Minutes from "Greater Works," 2017 was Moderator Williams's report. (1) Greenbriar Children's Center received donations for capital improvement. (2) Daniel Brown with a GPA of 2.8 received a full scholarship to Shaw University. (3) The Berean and the American Red Cross partnership during hurricane Matthew.

(4) Partnership with the Central Labor Council. (5) Support for truck drivers and bus drivers with a resolution by the Social/Civic Committee. (6) Randy Brown, State President, Teamsters Union, gave remarks.

President Timothy Sheppard, Congress of Christian Education, announced the increase in GPA to receive the Berean Scholarship from a 2.5 to a 2.7. The average must be maintained for one year or the scholarship will be rescinded. Scholarship will be awarded yearly ("Greater Works," 2017).

Sis. Carolyn B. Scott's email Minutes, November 14, 2022, report the following about the 117th Berean Missionary Baptist Association, Inc. Annual Session, held at Second Arnold Baptist Church, greetings by Pastor Richard Hall, Sr. Moderator Clarence Williams' theme, "Greater Works." The Session was held October 12, 2017 - October 14, 2017, Official Opening, Friday, October 13, 2017 – 9am.

The Minutes include the officers of the 117th Annual Session: Moderator Clarence Williams, Jr., Rev. Richard Hall, Sr., Vice Moderator, Sis. Evelyn Green, Women's Auxiliary President, Rev. Timothy M. Sheppard, Congress President, Dea. Julius Green, Laymen's Auxiliary President, Rev. Michael Stamps, Clerk, Sis. Carolyn Scott, Secretary.

Strategic Planning, Youth Violence, and Supporting Saints in Business were among the many topics that were shared at the Annual Session. The Strategic Planning Committee, Chairman Edward Chisolm, worked on a vision statement for the Association.

Children and youth activities were held Saturday, October 14, 2017, and children's registration was included in the church's registration, $150. October 12, 2017: Registration – Executive Board Meeting – 6:00 p.m.; Welcome Program & Musical – 7:00 p.m.

Moderator Williams opened the Session, and Moderator Emeritus Rev. Matthew Southall Brown, Sr. remarked, "Greater Works, Being a Voice, not an Echo."

The Minutes indicated reports were given. The Congress President, Rev. Timothy Sheppard, thanked Kingdom Life Christian Fellowship, Pastor Charles P. Roberson, Sr., for hosting the previous Congress. His focus for Congress is young adults. The Congress is looking to add the positions of Secretary and Director General. Congress is in the process of changing dates of Congress from July to June and shortening the days.

Dean Kathy Morgan gave thanks and announced COPP (Certificate of Progress Program) Classes. There are 8 Christian leadership schools in Savannah. As a result of their certifications, students do not have to attend state and national classes.

Laymen's Auxiliary – President Julius Green solicitated prayers from members for younger men to join. Mr. Edward Chisolm was the presenter for men.

The Business of the Session continued. Rev. Dr. C. MeGill Brown resigned as 2nd Vice Moderator. Therefore, Moderator Clarence Williams presented two names for 2nd Vice Moderator: Rev. Willie Rice and Rev. Andre Osborne. Rev. Andre Osborne was selected. Senior Saints, Rev. Carolyn Dowse, Coordinator, planned trip for seniors to Sapelo Island. The Association discussed the NAACP banquet and agreed to purchase a table. Members were asked to contribute at least $50 for a ticket. The Association also agreed to purchase a table at the Boys and Girls Club Banquet. The Association donated to Greenbriar Children's Center $1,500 for repairs. The Moderator proposed naming [purchasing] a building for the Berean Association, continuing the vision of former Moderator Matthew Southall Brown, Sr. to purchase a building for the Association. The Association Sermon was done by Rev. Paul Sheppard, pastor of Thankful Baptist Church.

Women's Department – Sis. Evelyn Green, President, gave her annual address. Prior to her address the deceased members were memorialized. Greetings were brought by Sis. Emma Jean Conyers, First District President, Women's Auxiliary of the General Missionary Baptist Convention of GA, Inc. Sis. Beverly Trotter was presenter for youth. The women held two fundraisers: the Agape Breakfast and Women March.

Highlights of Business Meeting:

- Moderator introduced Bro. Isom B. Harman, III and Rev. M. L. Jackson of Hinesville and Fitzgerald who are committed to the donation of $1,000 at the Congress in June.

- Members were asked to donate to Greenbriar.

- Introduction of Planning Committee: Bro. Johnnie Perkins, Rev. Carolyn Dowse, Sis. Sandra Williams, Sis. Stephanie Cutter, Rev. Paul Sheppard, Rev. Andre Osborne, Bishop James Rogers, Dea. John Finney and Bro. Edward Chisolm.

- **Vision Statement for Committee**: "Disciples Working in Unity for the Advancement of the Church and Community to the Glory of Christ."

- "Provide Fellowship, Training and Sharing of Resources with Member Churches to advance the Work of the Lord."

- 2020 Census was presented by Rev. Thurmond N. Tillman

- Needed training areas: Associate Ministers, Trustees and Finance, Children and Youth Ministry, and Funerals
- The Berean Association partners: The American Red Cross, Greenbriar Children's Center and Savannah Youth City, Inc. ("Youth Violence")
- 117th Adjourned Session at New Generation Full Gospel Baptist Church, January 2018.
- 118th Annual Session at Bethlehem Baptist Church, October 2018
- 118th Adjourned Session at First Evergreen Baptist Church, January 2019
- 49th Berean Congress of Christian Education at First Smyrna Baptist Church, June 2018

Holy Communion was observed, and the sermon was delivered by Rev. Thurman N. Tillman.

Sis. Carolyn B. Scott writes the Berean Missionary Baptist Association, Inc. 117th Adjourned Session was held at New Generation Full Gospel Baptist Church, Pastor Norris Darden, January 20-21, 2018. The *Savannah Tribune* states The Berean Missionary Baptist Association convened on Saturday, January 20, 2018, for the 117th Adjourned Session at New Generation Full Gospel Baptist Church, located 2020 Tennessee Ave., Bishop Norris Darden was host pastor.

Moderator Clarence Williams presided over the session, assisted by 1st Vice Moderator Richard Hall, Sr. and 2nd Vice Moderator Rev. Andre' Osborne. Bro. Edward Chisolm led an interesting session on 'Strategic Planning' (17 Jan. 2018).

The Adjourned Session began with the Laymen leading devotion. Moderator Clarence Williams called Session to order and welcomed everyone. The Host Pastor, Bishop Norris Darden, brought greetings and remarks. Moderator Williams announced Brighter Day Bail Bond is a partner of the Association. He encouraged members to vote and to join the NAACP. He announced the assignments for conflict resolution: Vice Moderator, Rev. Richard L. Hall, Sr., Rev. Thurmond Tillman, Rev. Matthew Southall Brown, Jr., and Rev. Lolita Hickman, the first woman to pastor a church in the Association. Bro. Jerome Irvin, President of the Central Labor Council made remarks and presented a resolution with the Labor Council which the Clerk read. A motion was made and seconded to accept the resolution. The resolution was accepted by body.

The Greenbriar Children's Center Director, Gena Taylor, Executive Director, thanked the Association for new lights in the gym. The Sermon was delivered by Rev. Joseph Hoze, topic, "Do you Have a Nickel?"

Dean Kathy Morgan announced class dates for Christian Leadership School and the Association was apprised of voter awareness.

Five Spencer White Scholarships were awarded to five recipients in 2017. A retreat was scheduled for April and Men of Faith were highlighted by Dea. Julius Green, President of Laymen.

The 118th Annual Session was held at Bethlehem Missionary Baptist Church, Rev. Dr. Wilson Scott, Jr., Pastor, October 18 -20, 2018. Moderator Williams's emphasis continued to be on "Greater Works." According to the 118th Annual Session Booklet, the officers were Rev. Clarence Williams, Jr., Moderator; Rev. Dr. Richard Hall, 1st Vice Moderator; Rev. Andre Osborne, 2nd Vice Moderator; Rev. Michael Stamps, Clerk; Sis. Carolyn Scott, Secretary; Rev. Joseph Hoze, Treasurer; Sis. Evelyn Green, Women's Auxiliary President; Rev. Timothy M. Sheppard, Congress President; Dea. Julius Green, Laymen's Auxiliary President; Rev. Matthew S. Brown, Sr., Moderator Emeritus; Sis. Florrie Screven, Women's Auxiliary President Emerita.

Clergy 2 Clergy Symposium, Strategic Planning and Social/ Civic Awareness are among the many topics that were discussed at the 118th Annual Session. Children and Youth Activities were held Saturday, October 20, 2018. The Youth Registration was included in the Church Registration, $150. Judge Leroy Burke, III, was the

Laymen's Presenter and Weslyn Bowers (Lady Mahogany) was Youth Presenter.

Moderator Williams in his letter to delegates, friends and supporters sought the breath of life from the Spirit of God to renew lifeless and powerless churches as a part of his welcome in the 118th Annual Session booklet. Among the topics at this session was the 2020 Census. The enrichment seminars included Clergy 2 Clergy, a discussion about grief, death; Youth Directors and Youth Workers, understanding Millennials in the church; and Evangelism, "they don't act like us."

Honoring Living Legends were recognized at the Community Engagement Dinner, Friday, October 19, 2018, 7:30 p.m. at a price of $25. The event was held in the L. Scott Stell Fellowship Building at Bethlehem Baptist Church. Entertainment was provided by comedian Big "E". The speaker was Otha Thornton, State School Superintendent Candidate (D). The Service was titled Honoring "Our Living Legends" in Religion, Education, and Civil Rights. The Legends were Rev. Dr. Sam Williams, Dea. Spencer E. White, Jr., Mrs. Betty Ellington, Dea. Floyd Morris, Dr. Carolyn Dowse, Mrs. Carolyn Blackshear, Rev. Matthew S. Brown, Sr., Rev. Larry Stell, and Rev. Dr. Leonard Small ("The Berean Missionary Baptist Association 118th Annual Session").

Included on Saturday's Agenda was the installation of the Berean Youth Council. Holy Communion followed installation and the Memorial Period. The Communion was conducted by Rev. D. Chavis, Friendship Baptist Church. Rev. Charles O'Berry was designated as the alternate.

Rev. Dr. Carolyn L. Dowse, Coordinator of the Berean Senior Saints Services presented a report that contained activities for October 2017 – October 2018 with projections for 2019 as listed in her report, Berean Senior Saints Services. The report:

Berean Senior Saints Services Benefits – (1) Provide training and support for churches desirous of establishing and/ or structuring senior saints ministries. (2) Aid in assisting with offering opportunities for holistic development of senior members. (3) Provide information relative to services available for seniors. (4) Provide opportunities for fellowship and socialization.

Summary of 10/2017-10/2018 Activities – (1) Free Senior Property Tax Exemption

Seminar: A free Senior Property Tax Exemption Seminar was conducted by Carol A. Osborne, Homesteads/Transfers Supervisor and Ophelia Allen, Homesteads/Transfers on Thursday, January 11, 2018 at Bethlehem Missionary

Baptist Church, 1008 May Street, Pastor Wilson Scott, Jr. Appreciation was extended to Pastor Scott and Bethlehem Missionary Baptist Church for the use of their facilities.

(2) Berean Association Women's Auxiliary will celebrate 18th Elizabeth Bolden Agape Breakfast on Saturday, May 5, 2018, at 9:00 a.m. celebration will take place at Happy Home Baptist Church, 1015 East Gwinnett Street, Bishop K.E. McNeal, Pastor. Our Theme: "The Power of Praying Women (Mothers)". Rev. Clarence Williams, Moderator; Sis. Evelyn Green, President (*Savannah Tribune* 4 Apr. 2018).

The Committee attached a Copy of Compilation and Analysis of Evaluations, the Financial Report, and the 2018 Older Americans Picnic Evaluation when they presented report at the 118 Annual Session.

(3) Older Americans Month: Annual picnic celebrating Older Americans Month was held at Tatemville Community Park on Saturday, May 19, 2018 from 11:00 a.m. – 2:00 p.m.

(4) Greenbriar Children's Center Christmas Gift Wrapping Project: Some members of the Berean Senior Saints Services participated in the December Christmas Wrapping Project by Greenbriar Children's Center.

Projected October 2018- Oct. 2019 Activities:

(1) Free Will and Last Testament Seminar: A free Will and Last Testament Seminar was sponsored by the Berean Senior Saints Services and Georgia Legal Services on Thursday, November 8, 2018, at New Generation Baptist Church, 2020 Tennessee Ave., Bishop Norris Darden, Pastor. The facilitator for this event was Attorney William Broker, Managing Attorney for Georgia Legal Services. Part of the publicity for this event included an appearance by Moderator Clarence Williams, Rev. Dr. Carolyn Dowse, and Attorney William Broker on the Mid-Morning Live Show on WTOC on Thursday, November 1, 2018 at 10:00 a.m. (2) National Older Americans Month Celebration: All churches were invited to participate in the National celebration of Older Americans Month by recognizing senior members during the month of May. The 2019 national theme and other pertinent information were distributed to the churches upon posting of the same. Plans for the Older Americans Month annual picnic for seniors, to be held at Tatemville Community Park, 303 Coleman Street, Savannah, GA 31405 on Saturday, May 18, 2019, were pending approval by the City to begin scheduling 2019 events. The *Savannah Tribune* reported that

The Berean Association Women's Auxiliary will celebrate the 19th Elizabeth Bolden Agape Breakfast on Saturday, May 4, 2019, at 9:00 a.m. The host church is Bethlehem Missionary Baptist Church, 1008 May Street. Theme: "Thank God for Natural and Spiritual Mothers". Mother Willie Hall will be honored. Sis. Evelyn Green, President; Rev. Clarence Williams, Moderator

(3) Health and Nutrition for Seniors Workshop: Carolyn Guilford, nutrition consultant, health and wellness advocate, author and workshop organizer formulated plans for a Health and Nutrition Workshop for seniors (6 Mar. 2019).

The report was submitted by Rev. Dr. Carolyn L. Dowse, Coordinator, Sis. Alvernia Jackson, Co-Coordinator, Deaconess Louise Bryant, Sis. Dorothy Davis, Sis. Willie Hall, Sis. Julia Johnson, and Sis. Joyce Brisbane Larry.

Secretary Carolyn B. Scott writes Berean Missionary Baptist Association, Adjourned Session, January 19, 2019, Moderator, Rev. Clarence Williams, 118th Adjourned Session, First Evergreen Baptist Church, Rev. Ronald Gregory. The Berean Association was visited by the following politicians: Mayor Eddie DeLoach, Alderman Carol Bell, Alderman Brian Foster, Alderman Van Johnson, Senator Lester Jackson, and other officials.

Other notables indicate that Sis. Emma J. Conyers and Sis. Ola Lewis were tasked to complete Sis. Ivy Richardson's history of the Berean Missionary Baptist Association. The New Generation Baptist Church was recognized for 25 years of uplifting Jesus Christ. Emphasis was placed on the 2020 Census, an awareness for members of the Association to complete census and for them to be heralds for the census cost. The Association served as partner to Parent University. A resolution was created by the Berean Association to address school violence, poverty, and suicide. The Finance Committee was charged to move forward with other ways of paying money to the Association, Givelify, charge cards, etc. Moderator Williams welcomed two new pastors: Pastor Vernon Galloway of First Union Baptist Church and Pastor Craig Daughtry of Clifton Baptist Church. The sermon was delivered by Rev. Norris Darden.

Moderator Williams listed the ingredients of a productive church:

1. Biblical Church working together
2. Celebrating communion together
3. Qualified Elders leading
4. Singing together
5. Maintaining discipline
6. Using spiritual gifts to bless one another

Moderator Williams discussed a business directory for members of the Association to list all businesses and added to this vision the following:

"Envisioning the Future Exceptionally as we Send Disciples for Christ" The Annual Berean Congress of Christian Education celebrated its GOLDEN anniversary in grand style. The congress convened at Kingdom Life Christian Fellowship (425 W. Montgomery Crossroads), Monday, July 8th – Thursday, July 11th, [2019] COPP and Certificate courses were offered. The 50th Anniversary Banquet was held to honor the trailblazers of the association July 10th at 6p.m. at (Central Baptist Church, Thunderbolt) (*Savannah Tribune* 23 Jul 2019).

For the third consecutive year the Women's Auxiliary and the Laymen of the Berean Missionary Baptist Association will deliver Gift Boxes to the Center for the Christmas in July event (*Savannah Tribune* 24 Jul 2019).

Resignation, prior to the 119th Annual Session, Moderator Clarence Williams resigned at an Executive Board meeting, April 2019. He served faithfully October 2012 – April 2019.

C. Moderator Richard L. Hall, Sr.

Sis. Carolyn B. Scott writes in Minutes. At the Berean Missionary Baptist Association 119th Annual Session, October 18-19, 2019, Greater Friendship Baptist Church, Moderator Hall presented the letter of resignation from Moderator Clarence Williams.

Rev. Michael Stamps, Clerk, called for a motion for Pastor Richard Hall, Sr. to serve the unexpired term from Moderator Williams. A motion was made and seconded that Pastor Hall complete the unexpired term through 2020; motion was adopted. Moderator Hall presented the letter of resignation from Moderator Clarence Williams.

The Berean Association of Churches 119th Annual Session leaflet introduced Pastor Richard L. Hall, Sr., as Moderator and described his emphasis: "Growing Healthy Churches," Acts 2:42-47, Teaching, Fellowshipping, Praying, Helping, Praising, Growing, Edifying, Equipping and Evangelizing. Pastor Charles Brown presented the Spiritual Enrichment. The Association required a new mailing address. The Association Sermon was done by Pastor Thomas Williams, First African Baptist Church of East Savannah. Prior to Moderator Hall delivering his Moderator's Address on Friday, October 18, 2019, an appreciation was shown to Pastor Clarence T. Williams.

The Berean Association of Churches 119th Annual Session leaflet also reports Youth Enrichment Sessions were held with their registration and lunch included in church registration. The partners were Savannah Youth City, Inc., Greenbriar Children's Center, Shaw University, American Red Cross, Savannah Regional Central Labor Council and New Generation School of Theology.

Secretary Carolyn Scott writes:

a. Moderator Hall asked churches to participate in the gala for Greenbriar Children's Center by purchasing a table at the annual banquet. Small membership churches were asked to combine to purchase a table. Moderator Hall is looking forward to churches helping churches.

b. The Moderator introduced Pastor Anthony Corbett, presidential candidate for the General Missionary Baptist Convention of Ga, Inc. (GMBC), who presented his platform.

c. A love offering was given to the past Moderator, Rev. Clarence Williams, who graciously thanked the Association.

d. Moderator Hall's inspirational message was taken from St. John 6:4-6.

e. Moderator Hall suggested registered churches should receive a Thank-you letter.

f. Moderator Hall's wished to have a youth to serve as Youth Moderator as a means for training young people.

Other Business

Sis. Patricia Henderson was selected treasurer of the Spencer E. White Scholarship Committee.

Sis. Sheila Arkwright contacted twenty-two inactive churches with the Berean Association to bring them up to date on the Association's activities.

Defining the Berean Missionary Baptist Association as a Baptist organization or as a fellowship of churches edifying, equipping, and evangelizing.

The Adjourned Session, in January, will be held at Litway Baptist Church in Thunderbolt, Dr. Leonard Smalls, Pastor.

Moderator Richard L. Hall, Sr., 119th Adjourned Session, 2020, Carolyn B. Scott writes Berean Missionary Baptist Association, Adjourn Session February 23-24, 2020, 119th Adjourned Session, Litway Baptist Church, Dr. Leonard Smalls, Pastor. Session began with Rev. Ricardo Manuel, Bible Study. Moderator Richard L. Hall, Sr. presented Nurse, Shirley Smith, who talked about the dos and the don'ts of sick visitation. Praise and Worship was led by Minister Johnny Perkins. The Sermon was by Dr. Thomas Williams (Obedient to the Mission (Ministry). The Association expressed thanks to host church and to Rev. Betty Jones who was filling in for the Pastor Smalls during his illness.

The theme for the 119th Adjourned Session was "Compassionate Care," James 5:14; Matthew 25:36. Monday's noon sermon was delivered by Pastor Roeman Bennett, First Smyrna Baptist Church. The evening service included Moderator Richard Hall, Bible Study; Deacons panel, Best Visitation Practices; and Compassionate Care Presentation – Hospice and Death in Home Visitations by Chaplain Jimmie Mikell, M.Th.

The Women's Auxiliary President, Sis. Evelyn Green gave remarks announced their activities. During Spring Break week of the public-school system, the Berean Association coordinates churches bringing children to the Bereans' designated location where students attend classes, have lunch, visit nursing homes, and have fun day on Friday. The Agape Breakfast, a fundraiser was scheduled usually in May. Sis. Debra Simmons, Director for Neighborhood Improvement Association, was speaker for Women's Hour.

The officers include: **Parent Body Officers**, Pastor Richard L. Hall, Sr., Moderator; Pastor Andre Osborne, 1st Vice Moderator; Pastor Thomas Williams, 2nd Vice President; Sis. Carolyn Scott, Secretary; Pastor Michael Stamps, Clerk; Pastor Joseph Hoze, Treasurer; **Women's Auxiliary Officers,** Sis. Evelyn Green, President; Rev. Barbara Simmons, Vice President; Sis. Willie Williams, Secretary; Sis. Denise Boatright, Treasurer; **Congress of Christian Education Officers**, Pastor Timothy Sheppard, President; Dea. James Green, Vice President; Sis. Kathy Morgan, Dean; **Laymen's Auxiliary Officers,** Dea. Julius Green, President; Bro. Raleigh Stephens, Vice President, Bro. Cecil Gwyn, Secretary.

The Association's website and social media:

Website: www.savannahgabereanassociation.org

Facebook Page: Berean Association of Savannah

Instagram: @bereanassociationsav

Email: bereanassociationsav@gmail.com

Virtual 120th Annual Session was due to the pandemic, Coronavirus, (COVID-19) and the recommendations from the Center for Disease Control (CDC) that in person gatherings be limited or avoided in fear of people contracting the deadly COVID disease. It was held nightly, October 21-22, 2020. There was no individual registration. Church registration was $150 to accommodate as many members as possible who wished to attend virtually. Wednesday was Youth Hour, 6:00 p.m. – 7:00 p.m. Min. JaQuan Oliver was featured in this hour. At 7:00 p.m., Rita Allen of Infection Prevention Alliance gave a presentation, "Thriving During a Pandemic." Thursday, Moderator Richard Hall gave the opening welcome; Min. Rita Futrell spoke on the "Toll of the Pandemic on Mental Health"; and Melinda Hodge of the Chatham County Elections Board presented a review of amendments in the upcoming election. Pastor Charles Brown of Greater Friendship closed out the session with the Inspirational Message. Members were directed to contact savannahgabereanassociation.org for more information (Green, "Berean Annual Session and Other Info").

The following people were thanked for a successful Youth Hour: Min. J'Quan Oliver, Dea. James Green, Rev. Barbara Simmons, Sis. Willie Hall, and Sis Elaine Snider (Green, "Berean Annual Session and Other Info").

The Savannah Tribune writes that every year the Women's Auxiliary and the Laymen's Auxiliary of the Berean Missionary Baptist Association sponsors [sponsor] an annual Christmas in July event at Greenbriar. The event is to be held on Friday, July 16, 2021. It will be a Drive-by Event because of Covid 19 (*Savannah Tribune* 14 Jul. 2021).

D. Moderator Andre J. Osborne

Moderator Andre J. Osborne 121st Annual Session, 2021, Sis. Carolyn B. Scott writes the Berean Missionary Baptist Association, Inc., 121st Annual Session, Host Church – First Tabernacle Baptist Church, Pastor Andre J. Osborne, Moderator.

Rev. Andre J. Osborne, Moderator presided. The theme was "MORE TOGETHER," Ecclesiastes 4:9 (AMP). At the morning session, the devotion was led by Minister Johnnie Perkins and the Devotional Message was by Bishop Thomas J. Sills, Pastor Connor's Temple Baptist Church.

Greetings and highlights at session:

1. Greetings, Pastor Richard L. Hall, Sr., Second Arnold Baptist Church and Past Moderator

2. Praise and Worship, First Tabernacle Worship Team

3. Memorial, Pastor Jerome Baker, Bethel Missionary Baptist Church.

4. Moderator Osborne asked for a Sacrificial Offering and Appreciation Love Offering for previous Moderator, Dr. Richard L. Hall, Sr.

5. Sister Evelyn Green, Women's Auxiliary President, presented her report and remarked on activities during the year.

6. EMPOWERMENT SESSION, Facilitator: Pastor Paul Little, II, Pastor of Bibb Mt. Zion Baptist Church, Macon, GA.

7. Deacon Julius Green, Laymen Auxiliary President remarked on activities from Laymen. They need additional members, and he requested each church to give him two names for the Laymen Auxiliary.

8. Sister Kathy Morgan, Dean of Congress of Christian Education remarked on activities from the Congress along with her appointment as State Dean of Records for the General Missionary Baptist Convention of GA, Inc. (GMBC). Sister Jessie Baker has been certified as Dean.

9. Pastor Gregory Thomas President of First District of General Missionary Baptist Convention of Georgia, Inc (GMBC) gave remarks and report on the state of the General Missionary Baptist Convention of GA, Inc.

10. Pastor Thurmond Tillman and Mr. Gregory Mitchell reported on the state of healthcare and gave a presentation on the Affordable Healthcare Act.

11. Mr. James (Jay) Jones presented information on "State of the Vote," and on Georgia SB 202,

12. EVENING SESSION – Pastor Thomas Williams, Vice Moderator

Remarks and Observations from the Moderator:

1. Due to the pandemic, Coronavirus disease (COVID-19) and Center for Disease Control (CDC), the Association's rules were suspended but continued with the Adjourned Session, 2022. All opening positions were filled at that time.

2. Intention - To establish a Recruitment and Reclamation Division that will also assist with registration

3. Continue Pastors' Committee

4. Strengthen Ministers' Division in Congress, classes

5. Encourage youth to join the Association and train and encourage seniors and youth to work together

6. Finance and Laymen openings, opening positions

7. Reestablish recommendation division, continue goals

YOUTH HOUR   Youth hour, (virtual) ages 11 and above, Presenters include:

    a. Minister Johnnie Perkins, Digital Media

    b. Minister Shannon Nelson, Depression & Self Awareness

    c. Dr. Jamal Touré, Social Issues

    d. Reverend Paul Smith, Healthy Living with God in Your Life

YOUTH HOUR   Group 2 Ages 5-10

    a. Bible Trivia

    b. Bible Story Time

    c. ABC's of Christianity

    d. Sing along session

Adjournment – Rev. Paul smith

The 121st Adjourned Session was held at Connor's Temple Baptist Church, Bishop Thomas J. Sills, Pastor, Rev. Andre Osborne, Moderator, February 26, 2022. The theme was "Together Again: Reconnected with God and One Another," Psalm 133. Pastor David Chavis, First Friendship Baptist Church, delivered the Devotional Message.

At Women's Hour, Sis. Thomasina White led the devotion. Sis. Robbie Brown, President of Mission at Connor's Temple welcomed the Bereans; consecration prayer was by Rev. Elizabeth Lucky; Expressions by Rev. Barbara Simmons; Greetings were brought from the Women's Auxiliary of the General Missionary Baptist Convention of Ga by Sis. Emma Jean Conyers, Southern Region Vice President; Income Tax, presenter, Sis Debra Simmons; Sis. Regina Thomas, former Georgia State Senator, was presenter, and she was introduced by Sis. [Min.] Brittany Barnes (Women's Hour Pamphlet).

The Congress of Christian Education, Pastor Timothy Sheppard, President, asked to save dates: Capers, Robinson, and

Daniels Leadership Institute, April 2022 and Berean Congress of Christian Education, Youth Session, July 6-9, 2022 (Congress of Christian Education Pamphlet).

Representative Derek Mallow, GA House 163 gave remarks on the state of the vote. The Parent Body's sermon was delivered by Pastor Brenda Allen, Abyssinia Baptist Church ("The Berean Missionary Baptist Association, Inc. 121st Adjourned Session." Handout").

There were several activities of engagement for Youth Hour. For ages 5-9 there were Zoom activities, ages 10 and above, Zoom forum. Activities for ages 5-9 included scavenger hunt, Bible trivia, ABC's of Christianity, Art project – United Working Together, A Moment in Black History, coordinated by Mother Willie Hall, First Tabernacle Baptist Church. The forum presenters for ages 10 and above included Mr. Edward Daniels, Mr. Cornell Heyward, and Dr. Letila Slay. The forum topics were Minority and Women Business Enterprises, County Recreational Participation and Youth Activities, and A Moment in Black History – The Origin of Black Churches in Savannah, coordinated by Dea. James Green, Zion Hill Baptist Church. Youth registration was included in church registration with no limit on the number of youth. The church with the most youth in attendance received a prize. Young people participating in the Youth Session were awarded a gift card.

The 122nd Annual Session of the Berean Missionary Baptist Association was held Friday, October 14 – Saturday, October 15, 2022, at First Tabernacle Baptist Church, Pastor Andre Osborne. The Executive Board: Pastor Andre Osborne, Moderator; Pastor Thomas Williams, 1st Vice Moderator; Dr. Richard L. Hall, Immediate Past Moderator; Sis. Carolyn Scott, Secretary; Pastor Michael Stamps, Clerk; Pastor Joseph Hoze, Treasurer; Sis. Evelyn Green, Women's Auxiliary President; Rev. Barbara Simmons, Women's Auxiliary Vice President; Sis. Denise Boatright, Women's Auxiliary Treasurer; Pastor Timothy Sheppard, President, Congress of Christian Education; Dea. James Green, Vice President, Congress of Christian Education; Sis. Kathy Morgan, Dean, Congress of Christian Education; and Dea. Julius Green, President, Laymen's Auxiliary.

Friday, there was a concert, the Evolution of Gospel Music, featuring the voices of Berean Choir and friends under the direction of Minister Johnnie Perkins and Sis. Johnnie Mae Holmes. The concert was on Friday evening, 7:30 p.m.

The Auxiliaries: Women, Laymen, Youth, Pastors, and Ministers held their sessions on Saturday. The Youth session was 9:00 a.m. for ages 11 and above. The topic was Inspiring Young Christians to Become Model Citizens. Retired Honorable Judge Leroy Burke was a speaker. For youth, ages 5 – 10, Dr. Latila Slay, Principal of Butler Elementary School presented a special interactive presentation.

Dea. James Green, Youth Director/Program Coordinator; Sis. Coy Williams, Youth Director; Rev. Barbara J. Simmons, Youth Advisor; Sis. Linda R. Green, Youth Secretary; Sis. Evelyn Green, Women's Auxiliary President.

During the Women's Hour, Sis. Gwen Burnett Grant and Rev. Barbara Simmons brought welcoming expressions and welcoming remarks, respectively. Martin Fretty, Director of Housing & Neighborhood Services presented a review of Housing status in Savannah.

Sis. Evelyn Green, President, Women's Auxiliary, delivered her Address.

The Parent Body Session met after the Auxiliary sessions. Rev Clarence Williams, former Moderator, presided. Moderator Osborne delivered the sermon, followed by Holy Communion.

Great emphasis was placed on voting at this Annual Session. Members were given directions to voting polls, how to secure rides to polls, and information on Absentee Voting and Early Voting. The General Election was held November 8, 2022. Bereans were encouraged to promote strong voter participation and educate voters on the Anti-Voting Law – SB 202.

President Green of the Women's Auxiliary reported at the 122nd Annual Session, October 2022 that the women did not go into hibernation because of the pandemic but the Women's Auxiliary moved to hybrid meetings and continued drive-up events. Dea. James Green coordinated youth session along with Rev. Barbara Simmons, Sis. Willie Hall, Sis. Patricia Henderson, Sis. Linda Green, and others.

World Day of Prayer for Youth was held in July. Young people prayed for the world. This day of prayer was shared via Zoom. Sis. Coy Williams and Sis. Vera Trappio coordinated the Youth Day of Prayer, a virtual event, supported by Rev. Barbara Simmons. Participating churches, Youth World Day of Prayer: Central Baptist Church, old fort; Brampton Baptist Church, Tremont Temple Baptist Church, First African Baptist Church, East Savannah; First Union Baptist Church; Zion Hill Baptist Church; First Friendship Baptist Church – Hamilton Court; Second Arnold Baptist Church.

During the Agape Breakfast, the women celebrated the lives of Rev. Carolyn Dowse and Rev. Elizabeth Lucky. The Agape Committee consisted of Sis. Doris Stewart, Sis. Dorothy Payne-Hill, Sis. Willie Washington, Sis. Tiffany Stewart, Rev. Barbara Simmons, and Sis. Linda Green. Participating churches with the Agape Breakfast: Bethlehem Baptist Church; Tremont Temple Baptist Church; Second Arnold Baptist Church; Clifton Baptist Church; Happy Home Baptist Church; First Union Baptist Church; First Friendship Baptist Church – Hamilton Court; Litway Baptist Church; Connor's Temple Baptist Church; Zion Hill Baptist Church;

First African Baptist Church, Franklin Square; First Smryna Baptist Church; Second Ebenezer Baptist Church.

The Christmas in July Project was coordinated by Sis. Linda Green and Rev. Barbara Simmons. This Project provides donations, cash, or other necessities, to Greenbriar Children's Center. Participating churches were Connor's Temple Baptist Church, First Union Baptist Church, Second Arnold Baptist Church, Zion Hill Baptist Church, Pilgrim Baptist Church, First Tabernacle Baptist Church, First African Baptist Church, Franklin Square.

The Congress of Christian Education report: Pastor Timothy M. Sheppard, President of Congress of Christian Education, at the 122nd Annual Session, presented his report, tentative plans for 2023 Congress: June 6-9, Children's Week; June 13 -16, Adult Week; proposed site, Kingdom Life Christian Fellowship on Montgomery Crossroads, Pastor Charles Roberson; proposed Congress Host, First Tabernacle, Pastor Andre Osborne; 2023 Class Offerings: The Role of the Deacon/Deaconess; The Role of the Youth Director; Church Policy and Polity; Rethinking Our Christian Education. The *Spencer E. White, Sr. Scholarship* is under Congress of Christian Education. The members who were present at the planning meeting were Pastor Timothy Sheppard, Congress President; Sis. Kathy Morgan, Dean; Sis. Gwendolyn Sheppard, Youth Coordinator; Sis. Carolyn Bryant; Sis. Juanita Harper; Sis. Gloria Mathis; Sis. Jasmine Grant, Sis.

Wanda Hopkins, Sis. Sheila Arkwright, Sis. Beverly Dempsey, Sis. Davita Cossey, and Minister Johnny Perkins (The Berean Missionary Baptist Association Pamphlet).

Sis. Kathy Morgan reported that the Congress was a great success, held January 29, 30, 31, 2023 at Central Baptist Church, Thunderbolt, GA, Rev. Timothy Sheppard, Pastor. The instructors and classes were Dr. Albertine Marshall, Christian View Towards Politics; Sis. Cynthia Hillery-Jackson, Safe Sanctuary Workshop; Pastor Vernon Lloyd, The Under-Shepherd; Evangelist Janice Johnson-Scott, Survey of John; and Minister Johnnie M. Perkins, II, Millennials in Ministry. Church registration was $125 which included church members' attendance (Flyer).

122ND Adjourned Session, hybrid, was held January 22 – 23, 2023, at Second Arnold Baptist Church, Rev. Richard L. Hall, Sr., Pastor, and on-line. The theme for the session was "Mental Health Matters." Moderator Osborne explained with the Pandemic, COVID-19, announced by the World Health Organization (WHO) in January 2020, the Berean Association did not meet in person for the 120th Annual Session but met virtually. For the 120th Adjourned Session, the rules were suspended, and the Association did not meet for the Adjourned Session in 2021 due to the continuing constraints of CDC. Several Board members resigned or went to be with the Lord, during this time. At this Adjourned Session the rules were taken off suspension. Bylaws were distributed and rules were to be followed.

"Building Healthy Churches" was the focus. The theme for this session was "Mental Health Matters." The Laymen's speaker was Everett E. Tolbert, LPC, Counseling and Consultant, LLC; the Women's speaker was Sis. Rachel Llyod, ED. S, LPC, NCC; and the Youth speaker was Dr. Deborah Heyward. The Devotional Message was delivered by Pastor Thurmond Tillman, First African Baptist Church, Square, Savannah, GA. His topic was "Saved for a Purpose," Colossians 1:9-10, Ephesians 2:8-10. The sermon on Monday was delivered by Pastor Roemain Bennett, Smyrna Baptist Church (The Berean Missionary Baptist Association, pamphlet).

Min. Brittany Barnes was welcomed as 2nd Vice President in May 2022, and the Berean women were actively involved in the First District of the General Missionary Baptist Convention of GA, Inc. where Sis. Green was appointed First District Women's Auxiliary President in November 2022.

The Women's Auxiliary Officers: Sis. Evelyn Green, President; Rev. Barbara Simmons, 1st Vice President; Min. Brittany Barnes, 2nd Vice President; Sis. Denise Boatright, Financial Secretary; Sis. Florrie Scriven, President Emeriti; Youth Department, Sis. Coy Williams, Chairman; Dea. James Green, Co-Chairman; Sis. Linda Green, Secretary; and **IT**, Sis. Jennifer Green.

At this 122nd Adjourned Session, the Board of Directors include Pastor Andre Osborne, Moderator; Pastor Thomas Williams, 1st Vice Moderator; Sis. Carolyn Scott, Secretary; Sis. Sheila Arkwright, acting Clerk until election in 2024; Pastor Joseph Hoze, Treasurer; Sis. Evelyn Green, Women's Auxiliary President; Rev. Barbara Simmons, Women's Auxiliary, 1st Vice President; Minister Brittany Barnes, Women's Auxiliary 2nd Vice President; Minister Tiffany Stewart, Women's Auxiliary Secretary, acting until 2024 election; Sis. Denise Boatright, Women's Auxiliary Treasurer; Pastor Timothy Sheppard, President of the Congress of Christian Education; Dea. James Green, Vice President of the Congress of Christian Education; Sis. Antoinette Ellis Ward, Secretary of the Congress of Christian Education; Sis. Kathy Morgan, Dean of the Congress of Christian Education; Dea. Edward Williams, Director General of Christian Education; Dea. James Green, acting Laymen President until election in 2024; (vacant) Laymen's Auxiliary Vice President; (vacant) Laymen's Auxiliary Secretary.

The Bereans, in studying to show themselves approved unto God as workmen who need not be ashamed, rightly dividing the word of truth in serving this present age, believe the work done and the work to come are their directives from Christ's Commission.

CHAPTER VI

CHURCHES THAT SUBMITTED A BIOGRAPHICAL SKETCH

Bethlehem Missionary Baptist Church

1008 May Street, Savannah, Georgia 31415

@bethelehembaptistchurchsava8553

Initial Pastor's Name: Rev. Isaac Brown

Present Pastor's Name: Rev. Paul Smith, M. Div.

Date Joined Berean: 1899

Joined Berean under Pastor: Rev. A.H. Harrison (1899-1902)

Hosted by Church, Known Dates: 1899, 1905,

1922, 1972, 1975, 1981, 1983, 2011, 2018

Bolton Street Missionary Baptist Church

821 Martin Luther King, Jr. Blvd., Savannah, Ga. 31415

boltonstreet@outlook.com

Initial Pastor's Name: Rev. M. W. Gilbert

Present Pastor's Name: VACANT

Date Joined Berean: 1958

Joined Berean under Pastor: Rev. W. N. Robinson

Hosted by Church, Known Dates: 1974

Central Missionary Baptist Church (Hitch Village/Old Fort)

738 Hitch Drive Street, Savannah, Georgia 31401

Central.mass.comm.ministry@gmail.com

Initial Pastor's Name: Rev. J. A. Evans

Present Pastor's Name: Rev. Tyrone Edwards

Date Joined Berean: Unknown

Joined Berean under Pastor: Unknown

Hosted by Church, Known Dates: 1951, 1974, 1978, 2011, 2014

Central Missionary Baptist Church

3119 Shell Road, Thunderbolt, Ga. 31404

centralmissionary1908@gmail.com

Initial Pastor's Name: Rev. William Dunn

Present Pastor's Name: Pastor Timothy M. Sheppard

Date Joined Berean: Prior to 1904

Joined Berean under Pastor: Rev. William Dunn

Hosted by Church, Known Dates: 1914, 1920,

2001, 2011, 2014, 2019, 2021, 2022

College Park Baptist Church

3301 Whatley Avenue, Savannah, Georgia 31404

CollegeParkBaptist@comcast.net

Initial Pastor's Name: Unknown

Present Pastor's Name: Rev. Andre` Young

Date Joined Berean: Unknown

Joined Berean under Pastor: Rev. Willie Gwyn

Hosted by Church, Known Dates: 1900, 1922, 1960

Connor's Temple Baptist Church

509 West Gwinnett Street, Savannah, Ga. 31401

ctemple509@gmail.com

Initial Pastor's Name: Rev. Noah Cornelius Connor

Present Pastor's Name: Bishop Thomas J. Sills

Date Joined Berean: Unknown

Joined Berean under Pastor: Unknown

Hosted by Church, Known Dates: 1976, 1979, 2016, 2022

First African Baptist Church of East Savannah

Initial Pastor's Name: Rev. E.C. Johnson

Present Pastor's Name: Rev. Cornelius Lloyd

Date Joined Berean: January 1987

Joined Berean under Pastor: Rev. Thomas E. Williams

Hosted by Church, Known Dates: 2009

First African Baptist Church

23 Montgomery Street, Savannah, Ga. 31401

http://www.firstafricanbc.com

www.theoldestblackchurch.org

Initial Pastor's Name: Rev. George Leile

Present Pastor's Name: Rev. Thurmond N. Tillman

Date Joined Berean: Unknown

Joined Berean under Pastor: Unknown

Hosted by Church, Known Dates: 1916, 2000

First Evergreen Missionary Baptist Church

622 East Bolton Street, Savannah, Georgia 31401

Initial Pastor's Name: Rev. C. C. Hayes

Present Pastor's Name: Rev. Ronald B. Gregory

Date Joined Berean: June 1935

Joined Berean under Pastor: Rev. E. A. Capers

Hosted by Church, Known Dates: 1945, 1954, 1957, 1960, 2019

First Friendship Missionary Baptist Church

506 Hamilton Court, Savannah, Georgia 31401

https://www.sambcsavannah.org

Initial Pastor's Name: Rev. A. J. Flewellen

Present Pastor's Name: Rev. David Chavis

Date Joined Berean: 1945

Joined Berean under Pastor: Rev. Galbert R. Conner, Sr.

Hosted by Church, Known Dates: 1950, 1976, 1981, 2005

First Jerusalem Missionary Baptist Church

4370 ACL Boulevard, Savannah, Ga. 31405

www.firstjerusalem.org

Initial Pastor's Name: Rev. Claiborne Curtis

Present Pastor's Name: Rev. Damion P. Gordon, Sr.

Date Joined Berean: Unknown

Joined Berean under Pastor: Unknown

Hosted by Church, Known Dates: 1944

First Nazareth Missionary Baptist Church

1023 West 44th Street, Savannah, Ga. 31405

fnmbc@comcast.net

First Pastor's Name: Rev. Sonny Alston

Present Pastor's Name: Elder Kelvin Green

Date Joined Berean: October 1995

Joined Berean under Pastor: Rev. W. N. Robinson

Hosted by Church, Known Dates: 2012

First Smyrna Baptist Church

1509 Burroughs Street, Savannah, Georgia 31415

www.firstsmyrna@gmail.com

Initial Pastor's Name: Rev. W. F. Underwood

Present Pastor's Name: Rev. Roemain Bennett, Sr.

Date Joined Berean: 2016

Joined Berean under Pastor: Unknown

Hosted by Church, Known Dates: 2017, 2018, 2023

First Tabernacle Missionary Baptist Church

310 Alice Street, Savannah, Georgia 31401

www.firsttabernacle1898.com

Initial Pastor's Name: Rev. J. C. Urby

Present Pastor's Name: Rev. Andre J. Osborne

Date Joined Berean: 1899

Joined Berean under Pastor: Rev. J. C. Urby

Hosted by Church, Known Dates: 1899, 1945, 1948, 1979, 2021, 2022

First Union Missionary Baptist Church

535 Berrien Street, Savannah, Georgia 31401

https://firstunionsav.org

Initial Pastor's Name: Rev. Andrew Jackson

Present Pastor's Name: Rev. Vernon Galloway

Date Joined Berean: Unknown

Joined Berean under Pastor: Unknown

Hosted by Church, Known Dates: 1907,2015

Greater Friendship Baptist Church

328 Tibet Avenue, Savannah, Ga. 31406

https://greaterfriendshipsav.org

Initial Pastor's Name: Rev. H. L. Heyward

Present Pastor's Name: Pastor Charles Brown

Date Joined Berean: 1998

Joined Berean under Pastor: Rev. Clarence Boles, Jr.

Hosted by Church, Known Dates: 2012, 2019

Happy Home Missionary Baptist Church

1015 East Gwinnett, Savannah, Georgia 31401

www.happyhomebc.com

Initial Pastor's Name: Rev. Cato Preister

Present Pastor's Name: Bishop K. E. McNeal

Date Joined Berean: 1899

Joined Berean under Pastor: Rev. Cato Peister

Hosted by Church, Known Dates: 1899, 1953

Mt. Hermon Baptist Church

Address: 911 Atlantic Avenue, Savannah, Ga. 31401

Initial Pastor's Name: Rev. Dorsey Phillips

Present Pastor's Name: Rev. Dorsey Phillips

Date Joined Berean: 2015

Joined Berean under Pastor: Rev. Dorsey Phillips

Hosted by Church: Unknown

Mount Zion Baptist Church

1008 Martin Luther King, Jr., Boulevard, Savannah, Georgia 31415

[www.mtzionbaptistchurchsav.ga.](http://www.mtzionbaptistchurchsav.ga)

Initial Pastor's Name: Rev. Edward Brown

Present Pastor's Name: VACANT

Date Joined Berean: Unknown

Joined Berean under Pastor: Unknown

Hosted by Church, Known Dates: 1980

Pilgrim Baptist Church of Savannah

P. O. Box 5032 Savannah, Georgia 31414

Pilgrimbaptistchurchofsavannah.org

Initial Pastor's Name: Rev. Clarence Williams, Jr.

Present Pastor's Name: Rev. Clarence Williams, Jr.

Date Joined Berean: 2014

Joined Berean under Pastor: Rev. Clarence Williams, Jr.

Hosted by Church: Unknown

Richfield Baptist Church

1415 Arcadian Street, Savannah, Georgia 31415

Initial Pastor's Name: Rev. Johnnie Powell

Present Pastor's Name: Rev. Johnnie F. Powers, Jr.

Date Joined Berean: Unknown

Joined Berean under Pastor: Unknown

Hosted by Church: Unknown

Second Arnold Baptist Church

1427 East 37th Street, Savannah, Georgia 31404

https://www.sambcsavannah.org

Initial Pastor's Name: Rev. H. J. Washington

Present Pastor's Name: Dr. Richard L. Hall, Sr.

Date Joined Berean: Prior to 1962

Joined Berean under Pastor: Unknown

Hosted by Church, Known Dates: 1962, 2009, 2017, 2023

Second Saint John Missionary Baptist Church

1323 Golden Street, Savannah, Ga. 31415

http://secondstjohnch.net

Initial Pastor's Name: Rev. J. J. Johnson

Present Pastor's Name: Pastor Antron M. Piper, Sr.

Date Joined Berean: 2005

Joined Berean under Pastor: Rev. Michael Lewis

Hosted by Church, Known Dates: 2017

Saint John Baptist Church-Mighty Fortress

2415 East DeRenne Avenue, Savannah, Georgia 31406

www.stjohnsavannah.org

Initial Pastor's Name: Rev. William Gray

Present Pastor's Name: Rev. George P. Lee, III, PhD.

Date Joined Berean: 1899

Joined Berean under Pastor: Rev. William Gray

Hosted by Church, Known Dates: 1899, 1902, 1907,

1912, 1913, 1919, 1920, 1922, 1977, 2008, 2009

Saint Thomas Missionary Baptist Church

1100 East Park Avenue

Savannah, Georgia 31404

st.thomasbaptist@yahoo.com

Initial Pastor's Name: Rev. Willie James Outler

Present Pastor's Name: Rev. Jimmie L. Mikell

Date Joined Berean: 2009

Name of Pastor Joined Berean Under: Rev. Jimmie L. Mikell

Dates and Sessions Hosted by Your Church: N/A

Thankful Missionary Baptist Church

820 Martin Luther King, Jr, Boulevard, Savannah, Georgia 31415

TMBCSavannah@gmail.com

Initial Pastor's Name: Rev. J. H. Edwards

Present Pastor's Name: Rev. Bobby W. Jones

Date Joined Berean: Unknown

Joined Berean under Pastor: Unknown

Hosted by Church, Known Dates: 2013, 2016

The Historic Second African Baptist Church

123 Houston Street, Savannah, Georgia 31401

sabc@historicsabc.com

Initial Pastor's Name: Rev. Henry Cunningham

Present Pastor's Name: Rev. Chauncy Blige

Date Joined Berean: Unknown

Joined Berean under Pastor: Unknown

Hosted by Church, Known Dates: 1945, 1982, 2013

Tremont Temple Missionary Baptist Church

1110 Martin Luther King, Jr. Boulevard, Savannah, Georgia 31415

tremonttmbc@gmail.com

Initial Pastor's Name: Rev. James Lee Dudley

Present Pastor's Name: Rev. Quentin J. Morris, Sr.

Date Joined Berean: Unknown

Joined Berean under Pastor: Rev. George J. Faison

Hosted by Church, Known Dates: 1978, 2014

Trinity Baptist Church of Savannah

906 West 36th Street, Savannah, Ga. 31415

http://www.trinitybaptistsavannah.org/

Initial Pastor's Name: Rev. Lolita Hickman

Present Pastor's Name: Rev. Gregory Ellis

Date Joined Berean: October 2013

Joined Berean under Pastor: Rev. Lolita Hickman

Hosted by Church: Unknown

Zion Hill Baptist Church

1720 Staley Avenue, Savannah, Georgia 31405

Initial Pastor's Name: Rev. Lymus Bond

Present Pastor's Name: VACANT

Date Joined Berean: Unknown

Joined Berean under Pastor: Rev. William Daniels

Hosted by Church, Known Dates: 2018

Epilogue

The Spark of Divine Intervention highlights the History of the Berean Missionary Baptist Association. As stated by the author, the late Sis. Ivy D. Richardson, capturing the history is intended to connect the dots as to why an Association in Savannah, Georgia was organized in Darien, Georgia. Hopefully, each reader will be able to empathize with the intense feelings and dedication of Sis. Richardson and the original committee in discovering the answers to the unanswered questions posed in her introduction.

Truly, I am honored to have been asked to serve as co- editor of Sis. Richardson's unfinished work, a work I am sure she would have gladly completed had she not been called to an even bigger reward by our Lord and Savior. Having known her almost all her life, I am fully aware of her unfaltering commitment to follow through in all for which she firmly believed. Both members of Tremont Temple, like our mothers before us, Sis. Richardson and I worked in the church closely together in many capacities. Professionally, she taught my son, and I served as her supervisor at both Sol C. Johnson High and A. E. Beach High Schools. When a task was needed, those seeking assistance knew they could call on Sis. Richardson for support.

Historian George Santayana stated, "Those who do not remember the past are condemned to repeat it." Although the reason for the coalition of churches that assembled years ago may have had growing pains, their focus today is the same. They still seek to energize churches and communities to engage in supporting spiritual and secular activities that teach our new generations what must be done to preserve past achievements and forge ahead. Unity in strength continues to demonstrate that much can be accomplished when we continue to ignite a fire, that spark, needed in motivating churches to define and enact those things to better serve the present age. Just as the forming member churches bonded together to prevent lynchings and other discriminatory acts, the work today that shows progress in our communities continues to positively impact today's culture when churches bond to promote acts such as voting and the teaching and learning of other skills. This bond demonstrates the need to serve and to provide an outreached hand to uplift those in need. It defines the opportunities needed to align with today's changing society. Most especially, the work demonstrates that we must continually engage not just our adult congregational members, but we must also identify potential youth leadership so that the journey started years ago will continue to expand in positively impacting our communities and serving as examples of the values and morals needed to demonstrate that it is God's guiding hand that leads the work in the Association.

Sis. Richardson used hymn writer Charles Wesley to say it best. "A Charge to keep I have, a God to glorify, a never dying soul to save, and fit it for the sky. *To serve the present age, my calling to fulfill; Oh, may it all my power engage to do my Master's will!* It was Sis. Richardson's desire that the young generation, through the Association's history and actions, will know the significance and importance of knowing their history; thus, youth will be more inspired to stay in the church. Those of us who were charged with completing her work hope we have fulfilled much of her desire and that her wish is just a prayer away.

Sis. Ola B. Lewis

Appendix A

A Workshop for Christian Leaders
Presented by
Pastor Emeritus Matthew
Southall Brown, Sr.

Berean Missionary Baptist Association
Reverend Matthew Southall
Brown, Sr. Moderator

"Study to show thyself approved unto God.
A workman that needed not be ashamed,
rightly dividing the word of truth."
II Timothy 2:15

Preface

We are Baptist because we believe that the Holy Bible was written by men divinely inspired and is a perfect treasure of heavenly instruction (2nd Timothy 3:16, 17) and that it has God for its Author, Salvation for its end (2nd Timothy 3:15); and Truth without any mixture of error (Proverbs 30:5,6).

We are Baptist because we believe that there is one and only one living and true God; an infinite, intelligent spirit, who is maker and supreme ruler of heaven and earth (John 4:24, Psalm 83:18, 147:5).

Textbooks used in this course:

Baptist Beliefs, E. Y. Mullins, Doctrines of the Bible

Daniel Kauffman, The Holy Bible, K.J.V. and The N.K.J.V.

Leadership:

"Whoever wants to be great among you must be your servant," Jesus told his self-seeking disciples. "And whoever wants to hold first position among you must be everybody's slave," Mark 10:43-44. When Jimmy Carter was the President, [he] told the Department of Health, Education and Welfare, "Jesus came not as first boss, but as first servant." Emory Bogardus's book, *Leaders and Leadership,* insists that true leadership rises out of traits, energy, intelligence, character, or religious principles.

Energy:

"Doers tend to rise to leadership." Proverbs 22:29, a man diligent in his business, shall stand before kings. Joseph served Potipar well and was made into an overseer (Genesis 39:4). Ecclesiastes 9:13 urges "whatever your hand finds to do, do it with all your might."

Intelligence:

We are not speaking about scholarly intelligence. We are speaking of a desire to learn. Know and understand, Proverbs 3:15; Proverbs 3:5; Proverbs 11:12. Intelligence increases by listening, observing, and questioning (Luke 2:45). "True intelligence finds its source in God" (James 1:3).

Character:

Character and Christian principles are basic to worthwhile and lasting leadership. Character and integrity go hand in hand. It's what one does and says, when no one is looking.

Qualities of Leadership

Quality: Something special about an object or thing that makes it what it is. Example: One quality of iron is hardness; Sugar is sweetness; Of Christianity, it is Love.

Leadership: In the word leadership, we see the word lead. Lead means to guide; to show the way by going along with or in front of. The star led the three wise men to Bethlehem.

Leader: A person, animal, or thing that leads. An Orchestra leader, a discussion leader, Albert Einstein was a leader in the field of Mathematics. Moses was a leader of the Israelites.

So, we can say that leadership is the position, function, or guidance of a leader, the ability to lead, or give directions.

A few years ago, *Time* Magazine featured 40 pages on the theme, "In quest of Leadership."

People from everywhere and from all walks of life shared their thoughts. Some defined leadership as "know how"; while others pointed to charisma, but the most definitions included honesty, vision, courage, and stamina.

President Harry Truman said, "A leader is a person who has the ability to get others to do what they don't want to do, and like it."

Field Marshal Bernard Montgomery of WWII said, "Leadership is the capacity and will to rally men and women to a common purpose, and the character inspires confidence."

The Bible teaches that true leadership comes through serving others (Mark 10:45). "For the Son of Man did not come to be served but to serve."

Leadership:

Ability, loyalty, sincerity, and sympathy, but it also demands moral and Christian excellence.

Joseph again is a shining example. He refused the advances of Potiphar's wife because he was determined not to sin against God.

A safe and true leader is likely to be one who has no desire to lead, but is forced into a position of leadership by the inward pressure of the Holy Spirit and the press of the external situation, Exodus 3 & 4, Isaiah 6; Jeremiah 1; Acts 9.

I believe it might be a true and reliable rule, that the man or woman who is ambitious to lead is disqualified as a leader. The true leader, called by God, inspired by the Holy Spirit, will be humble, gentle, self-sacrificing, and all together as ready to follow as to lead.

LEADER

L- LOVING

Because he has made the way at such a cost (Hebrew 2:10)

E- ESSENTIAL

Can not do without him (Phillip 4:19)

A- ABSOLUTE

Must let him lead altogether (John 21:22)

D- DIVINE

He knows the way (John 14:6)

E- EXCELLENT

Good company (Psalm 23:2-3)

R- READY

But all becomes ours when we accept him (Isaiah 48:17)

Baptist Doctrine

The Doctrine of the Missionary Baptist Church is unique because of our belief and our teachings. We believe that our origin began with Jesus Christ, and we teach that which Christ taught, the whole truth and no more or less according to the Holy Scriptures (Matthew 28:19-23).

The Bible scriptures are the fulcrum of our Christian faith. It is the medium through which God addresses man and the mean of man's knowledge of the incarnation, crucifixion, and the resurrection of Jesus Christ. It is imperative that the Christian leader believes the Bible, word of God, from Genesis to Revelation. Without such belief, man would be in danger of wrong extractions. Thus, the Missionary Baptist believes that the Holy Bible was written by men divinely inspired by God (2 Timothy 3:16-17; 2 Peter 1:21).

What do we teach about the ordinances of the Baptist Church? An ordinance in religious circulus is an established ceremony. In the Baptist Church there are two ordinances: Baptism and the Lord's Supper.

Now, what do we teach about these ordinances? We teach that both of these ordinances are symbolic. They are symbols of what Jesus did. Jesus was baptized by John in the river of Jordan (Matthew 3:13-17), (Mark 1:9-10). We teach that

Jesus commands that we baptize (Matthew 28:19). Water baptism can not save the sinner. The Gospel is enough to secure our salvation, John 3:16, 18, John 5:24, Acts 10:43, and Acts 16:31. The thief on the cross was saved without baptism, Luke 23:39-43. Baptism is a symbol, Romans 6:3-5.

The Lord's Supper is also a symbolic act of obedience whereby members of the Church, through partaking of the bread and the fruit of the vine memorialize the death of the redeemer and anticipate his second coming (Luke 22:19, Matthew 26:26, Mark 14:22).

The Baptist Church:

Baptist Churches must be cut from the pattern of the New Testament Churches, as set forth in the scriptures, in the principles, in the polity, in doctrinal, character and in Life.

The Great Commission is the program and purpose of the Baptist Church. It is also its task and creed (Matthew 28: 19-20)

Definition:

A Baptist Church is a body or company of regenerated persons baptized in the name of the Father, Son, and Holy Spirit upon the profession of faith in Jesus Christ; united in the covenant for worship, instruction, the observance of the

Christian ordinances. For such service as the Gospel requires recognizing and accepting Jesus Christ as their only and supreme Lord and law giver, taking his word as their only and sufficient rule of faith and practice in all matters of science and religion.

Church Discipline

The church is the school of Christ. As such, it should be controlled wisely and kindly disciplined. The church is also a family; let there be law and order in the household, tempered with tenderness and discretion; otherwise, the family fails of its mansion and becomes a reproach rather than a blessing to society. The church is the organic representative of the Kingdom of Christ; unless law prevails in the kingdom and order is maintained, how shall the King be honored? The Kingdom shall be advanced, or the world be blessed by its coming triumph? It is therefore of the utmost importance that a correct scriptural discipline be strictly maintained within the churches.

Disciplinary action on the part of churches is much less common today than it was some years ago. Christian people today are less willing to sit in judgment than their forefathers. Nevertheless, at least on rare occasions, discipline may be necessary and desired.

A. Three Laws of Christ's Church

There are three laws of Christ's house, royal decrees, given by him who is *"head over all things to the church"* which stand invested with all the sanctions of divine authority:

First, for every disciple, there is the law of love. "A new commandment I give to you, that ye love one another; as I have loved you, that ye also love one another" (John 13:34). This, if strictly obeyed, would prevent all cause of grief and prevent cold indifference to each other's welfare, unfounded suspicions, cause less accusations, jealousies, animosities, bitterness, hatred, and strife, and would cause each to love the other.

Second, for the offender, there is the law of confession. "If thou bring thy gift to the altar, and there rememberest [remember] that thy brother hath ought against thee, leave there thy gift before the altar, and go thy way; first be reconciled to thy brother, and then come and offer thy gift" (Matthew 5:23,24). This law makes it obligatory on everyone who supposes that a brother has [an ought] against him, to go to such a one without delay and secure, if possible, a reconciliation, whether there is, in his opinion, just cause or not for that brother to be offended.

Third, for the offended, there is the law of forgiveness. "If only thy brother trespass against thee, rebuke him; and if he repents, forgive him. And if he trespasses against thee seven times in a day and turns again to thee, saying, I repent, thou shalt [forgive him] for him (Luke 17:3-4). This law requires perpetual personal forgiveness of injuries, at least if those injuries are repented and confessed. It does not require that one has transgressed repeatedly should be held in the same esteem as before, for that might be impossible. In another form, the substance of this law was affirmed by Jesus, when in answer to Peter's question as to how often one should forgive a brother. [Jesus] he replied, "I say not unto thee, until seven times: but, until seventy times seven" (Matthew 18:22). That is, constantly.

B. The Scope of Discipline

The object and purpose of discipline is to prevent, restrain, or remove the evil that may exist, to encourage and protect the right, and cherish the good, "for the edifying of the body of Christ," that it may be "perfect in love, and without reproach" and that church is always held in higher esteem by its own members, and more respected and honored by the world, where a high standard of Christian morals is maintained, and a jealous watch-care is exercised over the faith and conduct of its members.

Discipline has a positive definite purpose: to heal the offense if possible; or, failing this, to remove the offender. If the erring one can be induced to mend his ways, the desire result has been attained; that is, in all ordinary cases. Some exceptions may be here after mentioned. "If he repents, forgive him" (Luke 17:3).

Examining Your Christian Walk
(Scripture References)

Genesis 5:24 An Enoch walked with God; and he was not; for God took him.

Genesis 6:9 Noah was a just man and perfect...and Noah walked with God.

Genesis 17:1 And Abram was ninety years old and nine, the Lord appeared to Abram, and said unto him, I am the Almighty God; walk before me, and be thou perfect.

Isaiah 38:3 Remember now, O Lord, I beseech thee, How I have walked before thee in truth and with a perfect heart and have done that which is good in thy sight.

1. How should we as Christians **Walk**?   ACHIEVED?

Galatians 5:16...Walk in the Spirit   _____

[The continued activities are missing]

<u>The Meaning of Conversion</u>

Jesus met a man who had an evil spirit. Jesus told the evil spirit to leave the man. The evil spirit left.

248

The Man felt like a new person. He was happy; he wanted to follow Jesus, but Jesus told him to go back home and tell the people how much the Lord had done for him (Mark 5:19).

Christians were often made to suffer. Peter wrote to encourage them. "Be ready at all times to answer anyone who asks you to explain the hope you have in you (1Peter 3:15).

These verses suggest two needs of each church member:
1. To understand his conversion experience
2. To tell others about his experience

Do you tell others about what Jesus has done for you? Do you tell them what it means to you to be a church member? Tell others about these two happenings.

Be ready at all times to give an answer. Say to them, "Come and hear all you that fear God, and I will declare what he has done for my soul" (Psalm 66:16).

What is the meaning of conversion? The word "conversion" means to change. A person is converted when he turns from sin to God (Matthew 18:3). He is "born again" (John 3:3). He is a new man (2 Corinthians 5:17).

Here are some scriptures that help: Ephesians 2:1-10; John 14:5-7; Romans 3:10-26; Acts 4:5-12; 10:34-43; 1 Timothy 1:12-17; Isaiah 1:18; James 2:8-26.

Tell a friend about your conversion experience. Ask him to tell you about his conversion experience.

LEADERSHIP QUESTIONS

WHERE ARE WE GOING?

A church requires a sense of purpose, a context, a mental picture of the future as a point of reference.

HOW ARE WE GOING TO GET THERE?

What organization is needed? What programs will we use? What projects will move us toward accomplishment?

WHO WILL WE BE WHEN WE ARRIVE?

Will we be able to maintain the integrity of our ideal self in the context of our future?

CAN WE FEEL GOOD ABOUT OURSELVES IN THE PROCESS?

Deals with performance and worth... and choices from a variety of alternative solutions. Fulfillment (of ministry) must be highlighted as much as priorities, goals, programs, etc.

Leadership's Limitations

Even the strongest leaders can't do everything.

People Limitations:

I cannot lead people longer than they're willing to follow.
I cannot lead people farther than they're willing to go.
I cannot lead people faster than they're willing to change.
I cannot lead people higher than they're able to climb.

Personal Limitations:

I cannot lead people beyond my leadership skills.
I cannot lead people above my level of trust.
I cannot lead people past my level of commitment.
I cannot lead people without my willingness to serve.

Appendix B

CHURCH LEADERSHIP SEMINAR

TOPIC: CALLING A NEW SENIOR PASTOR

Presented by: Pastor Andre J. Osborne, Moderator

THE BEREAN MISSIONARY BAPTIST ASSOCIATION, INC

And I will give you shepherds according to My heart, who will feed

you with knowledge and understanding. - Jeremiah 3:15 NKJV

PREPARING FOR A SEARCH

The call of a Pastor in the life of the church is a serious and joyful task. Sadly, in order for God to send a New Pastor, we will often grapple with the grief of having lost that which we formerly had, whether due to retirement, other opportunities, unfortunate departure, or promotion to reward. We must begin from this place of understanding as church leaders so that we properly account for the different sentiments that may reside within the congregation. There will be some members who grieve the old to the point that they feel unable to move forward. Furthermore, they may feel that the church should share this sentiment and halt the process for the foreseeable future. Advise them to consider Joshua 1, when after the passing of Moses, and an appropriate period of mourning, God urged His new leader and His people to move forward!

Congregational conversation may include:
- Is it the right time for us to call a Pastor?
  - It is NEVER a prudent time to be without a Pastor (2 Chronicle 15:3-4).
- With the current societal conditions, should we call a Pastor?
  - The current conditions mandate that we deploy Pastors who care and labor for the benefit of God's people (Ecclesiastes 11:4).
  - *John Gill wrote, "If nothing is done till all difficulties are removed, no good thing will ever be done."*
- Can we afford a Pastor?
  - Our churches can't afford NOT to have a Pastor. The church simply will not survive without consistent teaching and pastoral care. We should make proper preparation (Luke 14:28-30) and trust God with the resources He has given to us (John 6:1-14).

We must consider the emotional climate of our churches so that we prayerfully and properly get in position to receive from the Lord. We must address the various sentiments by assuring those members that their concerns are heard. Once we assure them that they are heard, we must encourage them to approach this unique moment in the church's life with faith. The call of a Senior Pastor must be conducted from the posture of faith. Consider 1 Samuel 16. When Samuel was to anoint Israel's 2nd leader, the first thing God addressed was that Samuel was to stop mourning for the former king, Saul. Considering the examples of the death of Moses and rejection of Saul, we can see that it is at times appropriate to have periods of extended mourning, but we must move forward when God says it's time to MOVE! Furthermore, God tells Samuel not to approach this by sight, but by faith! Consider 1 Samuel 16:7. Selecting a Pastor is a process that requires, we assume, the posture of faith and prayerfulness. We should be listening for God's leading so that we are pointed in the direction of the Shepherd that God has selected for the congregation. Therefore, before we do anything else, we begin the process by praying in faith.

The period in between leaders can feel like the wilderness, but God always leads His people through their wilderness seasons. Moses, Israel, and Jesus all saw God move in substantial and miraculous ways in their wilderness moments. Release your anxieties to God (Philippians 4:6-7), and trust that He will give you help and direction in the interim.

Prayerfully select an interim Pastor if one is available.

If possible, employ the use of a retired Pastor who can provide stable pulpit supply and care to the parishioners for the duration of the search. This person should serve with the understanding that their assignment will not exceed the length of time required to secure a permanent Pastor. If an experienced retired Pastor is not available, coordinate pulpit stability and congregational care with the mature ministers and deacons of the congregation to make certain Sunday worship and bible studies are being conducted and that the care needs of the congregation are being met. You should also seek the guidance/assistance of your association, moderator, and district leadership in ensuring your congregation's continuity.

THE SEARCH IS ON

1. Begin the Process with prayer, trusting God's promise to supply a Shepherd.

Several scriptures remind us that we do not find Shepherds/Pastors, but it is God who selects and sends them. Ephesians 4:11-12 says that Jesus gives these various ministry gifts to equip the saints for ministry service so that the Body of Christ is built up. Ask God to send the Shepherd that He has appointed to lovingly serve the assembly to which you belong. Pray that the church would follow God's leading and be sensitive to His selection. Consider Acts chapters 1 and 13.

ACTIONS: Hold a special time of prayer to petition God together for a Shepherd or ask Congregants to commit to personal times of prayer that God would send their next leader.

2. Commission a Pulpit Committee.

The church should prayerfully select a mixture of leaders and members to constitute a Pastor's Selection team to work alongside the Deacon Ministry in assuring the pulpit is filled and the church is given the opportunity to hear candidates meeting the qualifications. Members and leaders who are prayerful, faithful in attendance and giving, dependable, team players, mature, discerning, discreet, and patient should be selected for the task. ***Pulpit Committee members must not be persons desiring to impose their will or wishes upon the church.*** Pulpit Committee members should be trusted voices within the congregation so that as they report on the process, their thoughts and recommendations are respected and received by the congregation. Church leaders would do well to ensure the Pulpit Committee is a reflection not of different segments or factions within the church, but a fair representation of the entire church (all ages and stages). The Pulpit Committee should work with the Deacon Ministry and supply ministers to coordinate ministry from potential pastors within the church's larger schedule. This group should also be flexible enough to transition into a transition team to ensure the incoming Pastor begins his/her ministry with success.

ACTIONS: Create the qualifications to serve and set a date to nominate Pulpit Committee members. Set an additional date to present and commission them. Present them and pray for them.

Successful Search Committees will do the following:

- Lead with Prayer
  - One search committee member said the first thing she would purchase was knee pads.
- Select Officers
  - By the second meeting, a Chair, Vice-Chair, and Secretary should be chosen. The Chair serves as spokesperson for the team and ensures the committee follows the approved process. The Vice-chair serves in absence of the chair, and the secretary keeps the official meeting minutes.
- Review the Scriptural Qualifications for a Pastor
  - Committee members would do well to spend time in 1 Timothy 3:1-7 and Titus 1:5-9. If possible, get the advisement of association or district leadership as you review God's leadership paradigm.
- Review the Church's organizing documents
  - The search and call must be conducted within the confines of the church's governing documents. The Committee should be aware of the stipulations of a call, such as when and how the call is extended and the percentage of congregational affirmation needed to extend a call.
- Establish Guiding Standards
  - Early on, committee members must agree to common behaviors such as what is considered confidential, unanimous recommendations from the committee, and regular communication with the congregation through an established process.

3. Conduct Congregational Surveys

This is an opportunity for the congregation to give input on their perceived needs. The congregation should take into account the scriptures that outline God's standards for ministers. Surveys can be distributed in-person or via email and requested back on a predetermined date. In addition to survey responses, leaders should build a church profile that displays the current membership, current church demographics (age, gender info), history, etc. This information allows potential candidates to interview the church while they are being interviewed. Survey responses from the congregation will help the search committee to form a Pastor's profile. After congregational review and approval, the profile can be released via the church's communication channels, local outlets, the association, and the GMBC website.

ACTIONS: Conduct congregational surveys and build Pastor's profile. After building the Pastor's profile, review the profile, announcement, deadlines, and process with the congregation. After congregational affirmation, publish advertisements that include Pastor's profile along with requests for resumes and sermon audio or video to notify others of the search.

4. Receive and Review Submissions

The profile that was compiled using scriptural qualifications and responses from the congregation create the guidelines for reviewing resumes. Search Committee members are prayerfully identifying candidates with the qualities, character, and competencies that will enable them to pastor successfully in your congregational context. It may also be prudent to ask other Pastors, Association leaders, and Convention leaders for recommendations of persons whose resumes you should receive. *Release the announcement with a date that resume submissions are due by!* After the deadline passes, resumes should be reviewed by the Search Committee in the order received. Committee members may need a few meetings to review, consider, and prioritize the candidates with the most congruity to the church's profile. Once the number of resumes has been narrowed to 10, Committee members should listen to sermon audio/video submissions. At the point, the Committee should pause and pray for God's guidance in next steps. The Committee should meet again to prayerfully narrow the number of applicants to 5. At this point, resumes not considered should receive a response via email. The 5 considered candidates should receive the church profile. Also, the Committee should schedule dates to conduct interviews with the candidates. Get to know the candidates personally. Giving candidates the church profile allows them to ask questions of the interviewer concerning the church. The goal of the interview process is to narrow the top 5 down to 3, considering their preaching, administration, and effectiveness in their current context.

ACTIONS: Receive and review resumes. Prioritize resumes and prayerfully narrow to 10. Listen to sermons by the 10 and identify the top 5 candidates. Respond via email to all resumes received. Send church profiles to top 5 candidates and conduct interviews. Narrow top 5 to 3 finalists and present findings to the church.

5. Invite top 3 candidates to be heard by the church
An additional interview should be conducted to determine the candidate's pastoral temperament and philosophy of ministry. It would be wise to request references and also to interview the pastor's companion. *REMEMBER: the church is not the Pastor's bride, the church is Jesus' bride; therefore, the congregation should always support the Pastor's primary ministry to his family!* The Search Committee can create confidentiality agreements that will allow the Committee to familiarize candidates with the church's governing policies to ensure they agree. Candidates should also be invited to minister and to be compensated accordingly. The Committee should also conduct thorough background checks, criminal history checks, reference checks, verify all information, etc. It would be prudent to alert the church when candidates are ministering so that members are present, connected, and able to hear them. Also, it would be wise

to ensure the church hears each candidate twice at minimum. It would also be prudent to coordinate hearing the candidate in times of preaching/passionate proclamation and teaching/didactic instruction. The Committee should find a place to release candidates' profiles to the congregation that will give the membership a thorough view of the candidates' qualifications for this high call. In scheduling, the Committee should be considerate of other assignments the preacher may have, specifically if the candidate being interviewed currently pastors another church.

ACTIONS: For the top 3 candidates, arrange additional interviews, receive reference lists, invite them to preach and teach, and give the congregation as much information concerning them as possible. Encourage the congregation to keep their church's candidate considerations within the congregation. Conduct necessary background and criminal history checks. Committee members should visit the candidates' current churches, if possible.

6. Conduct a Final Vote

Start with Much Prayer! There are two ways to select your final candidate for Pastor (If this is not specified in your governing documents, this should be decided prior to the start of the search process). Primarily, the Search Committee, sensing the tone and temperature of the congregation, and having conducted extensive checks and interviews, should recommend the best candidate to the congregation for a ¾ (or whatever your governing documents require) affirmative vote by the congregation. Secondarily, all 3 candidates can be presented for a vote with the candidate receiving a ¾ affirmative vote from the congregation being selected. The reason one candidate presented is the best way is so that a minister is never invited into a split congregation. The selection of the Pastor should not merely pass with a simple majority vote. The Pastor needs the entire congregation's support. Voting can be done by secret ballot, at a meeting called for the purpose of electing a Pastor. If voting is conducted by secret ballot, the number of members and votes must match, a quorum must be established, the secretary should affirm that all present are members in good standing, and a trusted outside party, preferably the association, should conduct the vote, counting in the presence of all in attendance. Infirmed and homebound members can remit a sealed and signed ballot through their assigned deacon. Once the election concludes, the Pastor-Elect should be announced to all in attendance and the Chair of Deacons should communicate the Church's God-led request to the selected candidate. Before public announcement, the Deacon Chair and Search Committee Chair should have the candidate's agreement to come and serve. Then, they should follow-up with a formal letter, signed by the Deacon chair, Search Committee chair, and Church Clerk, expressing the church's belief that it is the Lord's will that the candidate become their Pastor with an immediate follow-up to discuss the pay schedule. The candidates who are no longer under consideration should receive a written response from the Search Committee.

ACTIONS: Pray and conduct the election. Alert the candidate selected and your moderator of the church's determination. Receive confirmation that the call is received by the candidate and send a formal letter expressing the call and the agreed upon starting date. Schedule an immediate follow-up to discuss salary. Send written correspondence to the candidates no longer under consideration.

THE WAIT IS OVER

7. Welcome God's Servant and Support him or her in the Task
The Pastor Search Committee should be thanked and commended as they become the Transition Team. The Transition Team will serve to assist the Pastor with becoming acclimated to the congregation and the community. The Deacon Ministry and Transition Team should work to assist the Pastor with arranging the Pastoral Installation. The Pastor holds the primary right to plan the Installation Service. The church leadership should express the ways to support the Pastoral Installation Service and to be completely cooperative in

supplying whatever is necessary and prudent to ensure its success. The Transition team could plan a series of meet and greet in the interim to help the congregation and community get to know their new Pastor in a better way. The Transition Team can help the Pastor's cause by being an advocate and helping him/her to get completely oriented and acclimated.

For further information or templates of any needed document, feel free to reach out to me via email at Pastor@FirstTabernacle1898.com. You can also call my office 912.232.5865.

Appendix C

INSTALLATION OF MODERATOR TEMPLATE

CHARGE - MODERATOR

Leader: Today, we begin a new era in the Berean Missionary Baptist Association, Inc. as we install _____ as Moderator. As the outgoing Moderator of the Berean Missionary Baptist Association, Inc., I charge you first, to lead this Association with the love of God in your heart. DO YOU ACCEPT THIS CHARGE?

Moderator – Elect: I DO

Leader: I charge you *secondly* to be an example for the Association Holiness. DO YOU ACCEPT THIS CHARGE?

Moderator – Elect: I DO

Leader: I charge you *thirdly* to conduct the business of the Association with integrity and Christian ethics. DO YOU ACCEPT THIS CHARGE?

Moderator – Elect: I DO

Leader: BY THE AUTHORITY OF THE ALMIGHTY GOD, I do now declare you _____, Moderator of the Berean Missionary Baptist Association, Inc. on the _____day of _____ in the year of our Lord AD _____

CHARGE – BEREAN ASSOCIATION

Leader: Today we begin a new era in the Berean Missionary Baptist Association, Inc. as we install _____ as Moderator. I charge this Association to *first* of all accept him as our new leader and to follow his leadership. DO YOU ACCEPT THIS CHARGE?

Association: WE DO

Leader: I charge you *secondly* to pray for the Association and the task of our new Moderator to continue moving us forward spiritually, financially, and numerically. DO YOU ACCEPT THIS CHARGE?

Association: WE DO

Leader: I charge you *thirdly* to be an association that is open to new ways of evangelizing the lost, equipping the saints, and strengthening our member churches to do effective ministry. DO YOU ACCEPT THIS CHARGE?

Association: WE DO

ALL: Moderator _____, we are ready to do the business of the Association and to follow you as you follow Christ. **Hallelujah!**

Used in 2013

Appendix D

Brief Overview of the Laymen's Auxiliary from Dea. Julius Green

The following statements reflect the work of the Laymen's Auxiliary in the Berean Association under Dea. Julius Green of First African Baptist Church of East Savannah.

Dea. Green was appointed to his position under Moderator Rev. Clarence Teddy Williams and resigned this position at the beginning of 2023 due to family health issues. Dea. James Green of Zion Hill Baptist, Vice President of the Laymen's Association, will assist until a new chair is named.

Prior to departing his office, he [Moderator Williams] and Dea. James Green were in conversation on having young men in the association train under St. Paul's Masonry School. Dea. James Green states that he is presently working closely with Sis. Kathy Morgan in continuing programs.

To provide assistance for the development of the Berean History, Dea. Julius Green provided information that might be used for review and inclusion in the publication of the Berean History. The information below represents activities in which the Laymen were engaged. Several activities were limited due to Covid.

- ➤ Assisted Berean's Women's Auxiliary in sponsoring and preparing for Greenbriar's Christmas in July.

- ➤ Laymen painted Greenbriar and aided in gardening to enhance the facility.

- ➤ Laymen Organization was a sponsor and leader in the Berean's Spring Break project. This is a 3-4 day event which provides recreation and sets up games and enhancement activities for the youth during the summer session.

- ➤ Set up programs during annual and adjourned sessions.

- ➤ Several speakers were brought in to provide information to young males. Among them were:
  - Pastor Thomas Williams
  - Judge LeRoy Burke
  - Several Police Officers
  - SCCPSS Police Chief

Dea. Julius Green noted that a session on mental health was recently presented by Rev. Andre Osborne on January 23, 2024.

What is most important as stated by Dea. Green is that the Laymen's focus has and should always be on ways to get the men of the Association's churches involved in order to bring in male youth into the knowledge of our Lord and Saviour Jesus Christ!!! He will continue to assist the Laymen's Auxiliary and will work with the next leader to encourage churches to engage more men in being active so that the support to the Association can be greater, and the auxiliary can accomplish its mission.

Appendix E

The Journey

Of the
Berean Baptist Association
Women's Auxiliary
1920 -1982

Part I

Sis. Florrie B. Scriven, President
Rev. Matthew Southall
Brown, Sr., Moderator

Preface

The journey is the report of the findings of the present Historical Research Committee appointed by President Florrie B. Scriven of the Women's Auxiliary of the Berean Baptist Association, Inc.

In 1965, a committee was appointed to research the beginnings of this Auxiliary with the objective of bringing the Historical Information up to date as far as possible. The report was presented on August 10, 1967. The members of that committee were Sis. Lula L. Allen, Chairman; Sis. Marie D. Green, President; Sis. Lillie T. Lewis, Recorder; Sis. Marie Milton.

This report was found with papers entrusted to one of our former Recording Secretaries, Sis. Irene Polite, who graciously passed it to the present committee for its use here.

We have edited and tried to put the services of the various sisters in chronological order but cannot guarantee its correctness.

The information on the Berean Academy was found in the Colored City Directory. The first mention found was in 1924 and the last in 1937.

We hope this will prove a boon to our self-esteem, for it proves we have been "somebody of worth" down through the years. The Committee:

> Sis. Janie B. Bowers
>
> Sis. Edna Dingle
>
> Sis. Jessie Gibbs
>
> Sis. Josie Mattis
>
> Sis. Betty West
>
> Sis. Lillian Spencer, Chairman

Beginnings 1920 -1967

Around 1900 a group of churches and their Pastors, probably some faithful Deacons and members, finding themselves having common interest, decided to associate themselves together to form an organization where they would meet annually to fellowship with each other and pursue the support of missions and education.

In 1920, our God allowed the organization of this Women's Auxiliary of the Berean Baptist Association, through the efforts of a group of zealous women and the inspiration of Rev. William Gray, the Moderator of the Association and Pastor of St. John Baptist Church at that time, to be organized.

Prayerfully, the group of workers was called together in July, which was then the month for the Annual Meeting. They met in Waycross, GA at a church then pastored by Rev. Starling. Rev. William Gray, Moderator and Pastor of St. John Baptist Church, assisted by Rev. Priester, then Pastor of Happy Home Baptist Church, presided and the first election of officers was held.

The following sisters among others were present:

Sisters: E. Dennis Perry, M.M. Mills (1st Bryan, Savannah); Chattie Sims, Alice Brown, Mollie Brown (St. John, Savannah); J.S. Moody (1st Tabernacle, Savannah); M. S. Grant (Grace, Darien); Ellen Brown,

Mary G. Johnson (Bethlehem, Savannah); Mary Major (White Oak, Monteith); Anna Maxwell (1st Bryan); Lizzie Cox (1st Jerusalem).

The first slate of officers:

President – **Sister M. M. Mills** – First Bryan Baptist Church

First Vice President – Sister Chattie Sims – St. John Baptist Church

Second Vice President – Sister J. S. Moody – First Tabernacle Baptist Church

Third Vice President – Sister Mary Major – White Oak Baptist Church, Monteith, GA

Secretary – Sister Emma D. Perry, First Bryan Church

Treasurer – Sister Ellen Brown, Bethlehem Baptist Church

Correspondence Secretary – Sister M. S. Grant, Grace Baptist Church, Darien, GA

This slate of officers served progressively for four years. Then, Sis. Mills was called to meet her maker in 1924.

At the following session (1925), which was held at Grace Baptist Church in Daring [Darien], **Sis. Dennis Perry** was elected president. (The record does not show who immediately followed her as secretary. Sis. Perry served successfully for 9 years and resigned because she moved to New York City).

Following the resignation of Sis. Perry, **Sis. Sarah F. Moody** (1933?) was elected president. Sis. Moody served two (2) years and resigned because of poor health.

[The Women's Auxiliary of which Mrs. E.R. Henrison is president, and Mrs. Thurmand vice president] (*Savannah Tribune* 31 July 1920, 1).

Sis. Carrie B. Thurmand – St. John Baptist was next to head this organization and served briefly.

Sis. Rosa B. Voss – 1st Bryan Baptist Church succeeded Sis. Thurmand and served as president for a short period. Sis. Voss is given credit for the organization of the Youth Department of our Auxiliary. She departed this life in 1962.

Sis. Inez Davis – First Tabernacle Baptist Church was the next president. She was not only efficient but dedicated, patient, and with deep understanding. She served faithfully until her health failed, and she joined the host of "homeward bound servants" in 1951.

Sis. Inez Davis and Sis. Bessie Foster (Bryan) served as teachers in the school operated by the Berean Baptist Association. The school was known as the BEREAN ACADEMY and was located at 11 Bouhan Street. The earliest evidence documenting the school's existence found was 1924, Savannah City Directory, Colored Section pp. 594; the latest 1937 when that address was listed as Berean Baptist Ch.

The following are reproductions of the listings for the years 1924, 1926, 1932, and 1937:

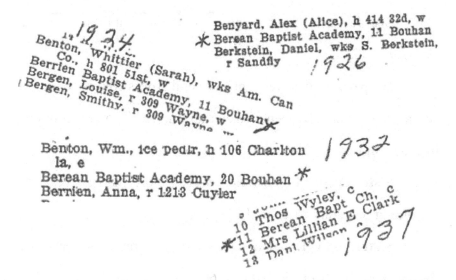

Benyard, Alex (Alice), h 414 32d, w
✳ Berean Baptist Academy, 11 Bouhan
Berkstein, Daniel, wks S. Berkstein,
r Sandfly *1926*

1924
Benton, Whittier (Sarah), wks Am. Can
Co., h 801 51st, w
Berrien Baptist Academy, 11 Bouhan
Bergen, Louise, r 309 Wayne, w
Bergen, Smithy. r 309 Wayne

Benton, Wm., ice pedlr, h 106 Charlton *1932*
la, e
Berean Baptist Academy, 20 Bouhan ✳
Berrien, Anna, r 1213 Cuyler

10 Thos Wyley, c Ch, c
✳11 Berean Bapt E Clark
12 Mrs Lillian
13 Danl Wilson *1937*

Sis. Emily J. Williams of Bethlehem Baptist Church was first president for the Youth Department of the Auxiliary. She was dedicated in her endeavor. Her passing in March 1946 was keenly felt.

Sis. Bessie Foster of First Bryan succeeded this devout worker and served with zeal for a brief period.

In 1952, **Sis. Marie D. Green** was elected president, after having served as vice president for many years. She was reported to be one of the few who "think not of the position, but rather the tasks to be done, to the glory of God." Sis. Green served for more than 20 years and was called to meet her maker in July of 1969. (Member of First Friendship Baptist Church)

Sis. Mamie T. Jones served as First Vice President to Sis. Green. It was with regret that she had to resign in 1968.

Sis. Jessie L. Stell – served as Parliamentarian. She was elected in 1962.

We pause now to recognize several sisters who have served courageously. Some have entered eternal rest – while others continue in a faithful way.

Sister Annie L. Graves – served more than 20 years as Recording Secretary (deceased 1962).

Sister Lillie T. Lewis – followed Sis. Graves as Recording Secretary having been elected in 1960.

Sister Mary G. Johnson (member of Bethlehem Baptist Church) served as Corresponding Secretary, later as Financial Secretary for a total of 29 years. She was also Chairman of the Memorial Committee when she passed in 1965.

Sister Lizzie Cox (First Jerusalem), served as treasurer with a clear record, served as pianist for a time.

Sis. Maggie Canty and Sis. Lillian Wilson – Auditors

Sister Alice Gordon, faithfully served as Treasurer for 20 years

Sister Victoria Roberts – Parliamentarian

Sister Lula Allen – Historian among other offices

Sister Rosa Johnson – Youth Directress

Sis. E. Dennis Perry, after returning from New York City, was elected to serve as pianist and historian which she graciously executed (Jan 1959).

Sis. Marie Milton, (Central Hitch) succeeded Sis. Perry as historian in 1960.

Sister Meta Glenn (1st Bryan) Chairman of the Board.

The following Sisters though not listed as officers, are recognized as having given faithful courageous service during the JOURNEY. Sis. Etta Williams Brown; Sis. E. J. Williems; Sis. Ellen Hogan; Sis. Julia McKenny; Sis. Prudence Green (1966); Sis Lillian Brown; Sis. Priscilla Hamilton; Sis. Sarah S. White; Sis. Sarah S. Moody; Sis. Frances Wimberly

MOVING ON
1967 -1982

Many changes came after the 70's. Sis. Marie Green, president of 20 years, passed away on July 8, 1960. We were unable to find any records of the years from 1967 – 1973. A new record book was bought, and we found no record of the old book or its location. What we record here is from this new record book.

The first entry in the new record book is of a Board meeting at the home of the President, Sis. Sarah S. White, who had succeeded Sis. Green.

Moderator Capers presided at the request of President White. Guidelines for assessments were set, and Sis. Irene C. Green was elected Assistant to recording Secretary Sis. Lewis. Approval for the purchase of a new record book was approved.

The slate of Officers in 1973:

Sis. Sarah S. White, President

Sis. Lillie T. Lewis, Recording Secretary

Sis. Fannie Woods, Treasurer

Sis. Maggie Canty, Auditor

Sis. Viola Robinson, Bd. Secretary

Rev. E.A. Capers, Moderator

The 53rd Annual Session of the Women's Auxiliary, October 11, 1973, was held at Oak Grove Baptist Church, Meridian, GA., Rev. J.F. Mann, Host Pastor. Highlights: Inspirational by Sis. Elizabeth Bolden; Information from Parliamentarian "Basic Duties of Officers"; The Youth Hour and the President's Annual Address.

The Adjourned Session of January 1974 was held at Bolton Street Baptist Church, Rev. T. Pryor, Pastor. Business transacted as usual. Sis. Carrie Rouse presented the Young People in a beautiful and inspiring program. There was no change in officers.

The 54th Annual Session, October 10-11, 1974, was held at Central Baptist Church, Rev. William Daniels, Host Pastor. Sis. White, presided for the Women. Sis. Eartha Lee Rickenbacker was appointed to work with the Berean Youth.

1975

The Adjourned Session was January 29, 1975. It was at this meeting that Moderator Capers submitted his resignation due to his health, and recommended the Vice Moderator, Rev. William Daniels be placed in his office. This was accepted by the Parent Body. Pres. White expressed regret for the Women's Auxiliary and moved that he become "Emeritus" and that the sisters would join the Parent body in honoring him.

A planning meeting was held on August 26, 1975, at Bethlehem Baptist Church. In addition to the business of the Association, Rev. Matthew S. Brown [Sr.] presented an African Exchange student. It was learned that the student was in financial difficulty. His mother had perished during the trip to the plane which was to fly him to the USA. The student spoke to the group in such a way that the Berean Baptist Association and the Zion Missionary Baptist Association and the Berean Women's Auxiliary took the responsibility to sponsor him and supply finance for him.

The General Session of 1975 was held at 1ˢᵗ Bryan Baptist Church October 9-11. Session proceeded successfully, no notable changes.

1976

The 1976 Adjourned Session met at First Friendship Baptist Church on Wednesday January 8. It was with deep regret that the women received a letter of resignation from Sis. Maggie Canty, because of health reasons. Sis. Canty had served faithfully many years as Auditor. Columbus, the exchange student, whom the Association had sponsored told of his progress at Savannah State College. Sister Luberta Burgress was named to serve as Vice President.

The General Session was held at Connor's Temple Baptist Church October 6-8, 1976. This session proceeded as usual. At 12:00 o'clock on Friday, President gave her address, which some called a sermonette.

1977

The Adjourned session for this year was held at Macedonia Baptist Church on January 26ᵗʰ. Rev. Levi Moore, Pastor. President White was absent from this session due to illness in her family. Special prayer was offered for her.

The President gave her Annual Address in her usual way. Session considered a success.

1978

The Adjourned Session met at Tremont Temple Baptist Church, Rev. George Faison, Pastor. The Women's Hour was at 2 P.M.

Sis. Sarah S. White, presiding, Sis. Fannie T. Woods presented Sis. Viola T. Robinson, Vice Pres. At-Large in the State Convention. She delivered a timely address from the National Theme: "His Peace, Power and Presence, Our Hope Secure." This was well received by all.

The Annual Session met October 5th. Devotions conducted by Sisters: Rickenbacker, L. S. Stell, and Marie Milton. The women's business session was well attended. The President gave her address, "The Service of Jesus." Other sisters who addressed the session were Sis. Fannie Woods and Sis. V.T. Robinson. The Association Choir rendered music.

1979

The Adjourned Session was held January 31, 1979, at Connor's Temple Baptist Church, Rev. Bennie R. Mitchell, Jr., Pastor. This session proceeded as usual with no major changes.

In an **Executive Board** meeting on August 2, 1979, it was decided for the 1st time in the history of the Women's Auxiliary that delegates would be sent to the Sunday School and B.T.U. District Convention, which was to be held at Elm Grove Baptist Church,

Meridian, GA. The delegate from the Women's Auxiliary was Sis. Marie Milton. President White was praised for this endeavor.

The 80th Annual Session met at Tabernacle Baptist Church October 11-12. Women's Hour Thursday. Address by Sis. Mary Johnson of Bethlehem, "Its Time."

The report from the S.S. and B.T.U. Convention was made by Sis. Marie Milton. The History of the Auxiliary was read by Sis. Lillie T. Lewis.

On Friday the President gave her Annual Address. President White spoke from her heart, subject, "God Will Take Care of You."

Two new ministers were introduced: Rev. Clifton from College Park and Rev. [Robert] Twyman from Mt. Zion.

The Adjourned Session was held January 28, 1980, at Macedonia Baptist Church, Rev. Archie Fields, Pastor. This session proceeded as usual with no major changes.

The 81st Annual Session met October 9 -11, 1980 at Mt. Zion Baptist Church, Rev. Robert Twyman, Pastor, Women's Session 2 p.m., President White, presiding.

At the time Secretary Lewis had become ill, though present. The Sisters decided to give her some help and elected Sis. Jessie Gibbs as Assistant Recording Secretary.

Sis. Henrietta Green asked to be relieved (because of illness) of her duties as Chair of the Ways and Means Committee. Her relief was granted, and Sis. Lily Wilder was elected Chairman.

President made a timely address with thanks given for all the support through the years. Historian Sis. Marie Milton made an interesting report of the progress of our Auxiliary. Sessions completed and closed in usual form, and no further changes were made to officers.

1981

The 1981 Adjourned Session met on January 28, 1981, at Bethlehem Baptist Church, 2 p.m. Women's Hour. The President was presented by Sis. Lillie T. Lewis to address the sisters. She spoke from the theme: "Count your Blessings." No one was present for youth hour.

The Annual Session met at 1st Friendship Baptist Church, October 8 – 11, 1981; 1:30, October 8th – the board meeting was held. Sis. Mary Matthews was added to the board and Sis. Jessie Gibbs was elected Chairman of the Board. Routine business was attended; 12:15, October 9th – Women's Hour, Vice Pres Nettie Merritt presiding. Following a solo by Sis. Bernice Green, Sis. White gave her address. Information on parliamentary usage was given by Sis. Stell. A thought-provoking address was given by Sis. Jessie Gibbs.

The President gave her Annual Address in her usual way. The Session was considered a success.

1982

The Adjourned Session met on January 27th 1982.

The Women's Auxiliary met at 1:30 p.m., fervent devotion offered by sisters. President White requested that State Vice President, Sis. Viola T. Robinson, enlighten us on the theme for the session: "Fulfilling God's Great Expectations Through Service." Sis. Robinson was entertaining as well as informative. The session concluded by continuing in the next service.

In a Board Meeting on September 21st the Missionary Societies' registration amount was raised after 20 years, from $8.00 to $10.00. Donations were given to sick members.

The 83rd Annual Session met on October 7 – 11, 1982 was at Second African Baptist Church. At 11 a.m. President White was assisted to the pulpit by Sis. Fannie Woods, at the request of Moderator J. F. Mann [the Moderator of Zion Missionary Baptist Association] who was presiding. The President was very direct in her remarks, and among other things asked that every member pray that she grows stronger. The rest of this session was conducted and concluded as usual.

The Berean's Missionary Baptist Association's Women's Auxiliary Presidents

1920 – 2023

1st Sis. M.M. Mills   First Bryan Missionary Baptist Church

2nd Sis. E. Dennis Perry   Grace Baptist (Daren, GA)

3rd Sis. Sarah F. Moody

[The Women's Auxiliary of which Mrs. E.R. Henrison is president, and Mrs. Thurmand vice president] (*Savannah Tribune* 31 *July 1920, 1).*

4th Sis. Carrie B. Thurmand	St. John Missionary Baptist Church (The Mighty Fortress)
5th Sis. Rosa B. Voss	First Bryan Missionary Baptist Church
6th Sis. Inez Davis	First Tabernacle Missionary Baptist Church
7th Sis. Bessie Foster	First Bryan Missionary Baptist Church
8th Sis. Marie D. Green	First Friendship Missionary Baptist Church
9th Sis. Sarah White	First Bryan Missionary Baptist Church
10th Sis. Annie Lizzie Ross	St. John Missionary Baptist Church (The Mighty Fortress)
11th Sis. Florrie B. Scriven	First Nazareth Missionary Baptist Church
12th Sis. Evelyn Green	Second Arnold Missionary Baptist Church

*All the churches are in Savannah, GA, except Grace Baptist

Appendix F

Spencer E. White, Sr. Scholarship Committee Information Booklet

According to the *Spencer E. White, Sr. Scholarship Committee Information Booklet,* the Scholarship Committee, Spencer E. White, Sr., Founder, was founded 1962. The motto is "A Mind Is A Terrible Thing to Waste" and scripture, "Let this mind be in you which was also in Christ Jesus," Philippians 2:5. The Mission Statement: The Spencer E. White, Sr., Committee's mission is to provide spiritual and financial support to students who have chosen to further their educational prowess at a post-secondary academic institution and who have shown exceptional leadership and responsibility in their home and Church.

The *Spencer E. White, Sr. Scholarship Committee Information Booklet* says Spencer Ellis White was born May 4, 1899 to Spencer Ellis White and Edith White in Sylvania, Georgia, Screven County. The booklet describes him:

Spencer was an energetic young lad who, according to stories by his elder sister Penny, showed great interest in being a leader. He began going to school, and in the second grade was told he could no longer attend school. At that time, he had to work the plantation on which the family lived. Not to be diminished by that, he continued to read and to study. Even then he realized the importance of acquiring knowledge.

After reaching manhood, he enlisted in the United States Army and served in World War I. He was honorably discharged from the army.

After his stint in the armed services, he returned home and got married. His first wife died shortly thereafter. He later met and married Ruth Hodge. They moved to Savannah and began making a life. They produced two sons, Spencer Ellis White, Jr. and Willie James White.

Spencer Ellis White, Sr. was not a slacker. Upon his arrival into the city, he immediately began working as a Plastering Laborer. He gained enough knowledge of the trade of Plastering that soon he was able to establish the first or one of the first black owned Plastering Contracting businesses in Savannah, Georgia. Using his business to bolster his family was not enough. He employed his brothers and other family members, teaching them the trade and thus allowing them to become independent contractors as well. He and his wife also were the proprietors of a neighborhood store on the corner of Anderson and East Broad Streets.

Business aside, Spencer Ellis White Sr., and his family became members of the First Tabernacle Missionary Baptist Church in the early 1930's. He was an active member of the church and spent much of his time attending local, state, and national Baptist conventions. His diligence in being a proactive Christian man was cause for him being named a Deacon and Sunday School teacher. Later he was named Chairman of the Deacon Board, a position he held for more than 50 years.

Running a business, working in the church, and yet, he found the time to become an active member of the Berean Sunday School and Baptist Training Union Convention, a body of local churches. He worked as hard in the organization and was later named President. This convention for him was an opportunity to train young people to become leaders in their respective churches. His dedication and interest in that led him to establish the Berean Sunday School and BTU Scholarship Committee. This committee would award a scholarship to participating young people who upon high school graduation had chosen to further their education at a post-secondary institution of higher learning. He made the first financial contribution to this scholarship. As the convention grew, it became known as the Berean Sunday School and BTU Congress of Christian Education, and the scholarship committee became known as the Spencer E. White, Sr. Scholarship Committee.

Deacon Spencer E. White, Sr. was called to be with his heavenly Father on Sunday, June 24, 1984 at the age of 94.

The *Spencer E. White, Sr. Scholarship Committee Information Booklet* presents the history of Scholarship Committee:

Lives of great men always remind us that we can make our lives sublime and departing leave behind us "Footprints on the sand of time." These lines describe the person who was foremost in organizing the Berean Sunday School and BTU Scholarship of the Berean Convention. His daily air was that of promoting Christian Education in young people. He nurtured this desire and one year before the convention became a congress, his dream came true. In 1962, at Second Arnold Baptist Church, around noon a group composed of Sis. O. B. Dingle, Sis Reda Butler, Sis. Annie L. Rickenbacker, Sis. Berta Rickenbacker, Dea. John Delaware, Dea. George Hayes, Rev. E. A. Capers, Rev. J.F. Mann, and Dea. James Rickenbacker assembled. They huddled in a corner in the back of the church and came up with an organization which was named "Berean Scholarship Fund," Sis. O.B. Dingle, Assistant Chairman, Sis. Reda Butler, Secretary, Sis. Berta Rickenbacker, Treasurer, Rev. J. F. Mann & Rev. E. A. Capers, Supervisors.

Plans got under way to raise money to give at least one scholarship during 1963. Pledges were made by the newly organized group. The first of 10 dollars was given by Dea. James Rickenbacker. By September 1963 from that seed, a scholarship of $100 was given to Miss Betty Simmons (now Sis. West), Dean of the Congress. In later years, the name of the scholarship fund was changed from Berean Scholarship to the Spencer E. White, Sr. Scholarship Fund. The Scholarship Committee met once a month at First Tabernacle, which was headquarters. Rev. E. A. Capers was the Chairman of the Scholarship Committee at that time. On March 16, 1963, Dea. White made two suggestions for the committee:

1. That a layman would always be Chairman and Rev. E. A. Capers, Moderator of the Association would be ex-officio of the Committee.

2. The Scholarship effort is that of the Association being sponsored by the Sunday School and BTU Convention of the Berean Association. The

Association would be obligated to contribute and sustain the effort particularly when financing was needed.

Later that year, Dea. Delaware became Chairman and new members were added: Sis. Alfreda Shaw, Sis. Ollie P. Grant, Sis Elizabeth Allen, Sis. Betty West, Sis. Rosa Pinckney, and Sis. O.N. Young. Sis. A Shaw was made Secretary and Sis. Viola Robinson was the first Program Chairman. Sis. Shaw was the third Secretary.

The Committee worked hard to help finance as many recipients as were chosen. Sis. Dingle became the next Chairman, and new members were added: Sis. Milton, Dea. Johnnie Holmes, Dea George Winbush, Dea. George Ponder and Dea. Clifford Hendrix. Dea. Hendrix was made Chairman, and during his reign, the following members were added: Sis. Thomasina White, Sis. Mary E. Hendrix, Sis. Frances McLaurin, Rev. Larry Stell, Sis. Gloria Ferguson, Sis. Patricia Henderson and Sis. Anne Clay. A vision was given to Dea. Hendrix to honor the memory of the late Dea. Spencer E. White, Sr. On September 24, 1986, a special program was presented and the family of the late Dea. White was honored. After the passing of Dea. Hendrix in 2001, Sis. Gloria Ferguson became the new Chairman, and the following members were added: Sis. Versie Dupont, Sis. Linda Johnson, and Dea. Willie Brown. Sis. Ferguson worked faithfully and untiringly until her illness and passing in 2005. Sis. Thomasina White became the new Chairman and Sis. Brenda Grant was added as a member. Since the committee's formation, we have had five (5) Chairmen and have given sixty-nine (69) scholarships.

Past and Present Chairmen:

Dea. Spencer E. White, Sr. .... Founder

Dea. John Delaware .... 1st Chairman

Sis. Ola B. Dingle .... 2nd Chairman

Sis. Betty West .... Interim

Dea. Clifford Hendrix .... 3rd Chairman

Sis. Gloria Ferguson .... 4th Chairman

Sis. Thomasina White .... 5th Chairman

Present Officers are as follows:

Sis. Thomasina White .... Chairman

Sis. Versie Dupont .... Recording Secretary

Sis. Anne Clay .... Asst Recording Secretary

Sis. Mary E. Hendrix .... Corresponding Secretary

Dea. Willie Brown .... Treasurer

Sis. Frances McLaurin .... Asst Promotional Chairman

Dean Betty West .... Evaluation Committee

Sis. Mary E. Hendrix .... Evaluation Committee

Dea. Robert Everson .... President and Executive

Officer of the Committee

Rev. Matthew S. Brown, Sr. .... Moderator

Sis. Brenda Grant .... Evaluation Committee

Sis. Linda Johnson .... Member

Rev. Larry Stell .... Chaplain

The *Spencer E. White, Sr. Scholarship Committee Information Booklet* presents the Berean Missionary Baptist Congress of Christian Education's Criteria for the Application for the Annual Spencer E. White Scholarship (A ward of the Berean Missionary Baptist Congress of Christian Education):

1. The applicant must be a member of a church that is a member of the Berean Sunday School and BTU Congress. The church must be in good standing with the Berean Missionary Association and be an annual Scholarship Contributor.

2. The applicant must be a person of good moral character.

3. The applicant must be an active member of his or her church, taking part in the life of the church.

4. The applicant must be a graduate of a Senior High School with a scholastic average of B or above.

5. The applicant must verify the records and standing in the school from which he or she graduated – by their transcript. A letter of recommendation from their church should accompany the application.

6. The applicant must be planning to attend a college of his or her choice the next school year. The name of the college should appear on the application.

7. The applicant must have his or her application in, on or before May 15th of the year of graduation.

8. Each year at least one scholarship winner will be chosen and recognized if he or she qualifies. The total amount of the scholarship will be announced; it will be prorated in four parts. If the student remains in college for four years and maintains passing grades, he or she will receive that allotment for the entire four years. Please notify Sis. Thomasina C. White or Sis. Mary E. Hendrix if you qualify.

9. When the scholarship winner matriculates in the college of his or her choice, and the Registrar notifies Sis. White, all checks will be issued at the Founder's Day Program in October.

How was The Spencer E. White, Sr. Scholarship funded? The booklet listed events that contributed to the success of the Spencer E. White Scholarship: contributions, fundraisers, sing-offs, youth night plays, bake sales, bus rides, raffles, 7 speaker program, candy sales, car washes, garage sales, dinners, t-shirt sales, roll call of churches, Founder's Day, banquets.

Persons Who Have Received Funds from

the Spencer E. White Scholarship

Betty Simmons	1963	Second Arnold
Lydia Smith	1964	Tabernacle
Leroy Wright	1965	Second Arnold
Marcelite Dingle	1966	First Bryan
Arelia Smith	1967	Tabernacle
Georgia Ann Wright	1967	First Bryan
Patricia Merritt	1968	College Park
Shirley Small	1969	Evergreen
Evelyn Wright	1968	Second Arnold
Ethel Hunter	1970	First African
Catherine Clements	1971	Central (Thunderbolt)
Allen Wright	1972	Second Arnold
Cosman	1973	Central (Hitch Village)

Audrey Gadsden	1974	First Bryan
Pamela Brown	1975	Elm Grove
Janet Jones	1975	First African
Pamela Rountree	1976	First Evergreen
Gregory Lockhart	1977	Tabernacle
Harold Leonard	1977	Tabernacle
Julius Hall	1977	St. John
Sara Elaine Wright	1978	Second Arnold
Jerome Williams	1978	

Denise Johnson	1979	Central (Hitch Village)
Freddie Mingledoff	1980	Union Baptist
LaTonia Jenkins	1981	
Leslie Smith	1983	
Rose Marie Lee	1984	
John Spaulding	1984	Second Arnold
Sheila Hudson	1985	St. John
Kevin C. Johnson	1986	Tremont Temple
Rickey D. Rivers	1986	(returned)
Jenee Polite	1987	Central (Hitch Village)
Reginald Lockhart	1987	Tabernacle
Ernest C. Maynor	1988	Second African
Stacy A. Bolden	1988	Mt. Zion
Sharon German	1989	Jerusalem
Roderick West	1989	Second Arnold
Kendra R. James	1989	First Bryan
Natasha Beckett	1990	First African
Sharelle Parrish	1990	First Union
Nicole Bryant	1990	Tremont Temple
Yolanda Johnson	1990	First Friendship
Adrian Jackson	1990	First Evergreen
Lorraine Copeland	1990	First African (East Savannah)

Appendix G

Bereanmba.org/join

Berean Missionary Baptist Association, Inc.

Membership Application

*denotes a required field

- Church Name*

  _____

- Church Address*

  Street Address: _____

  City: _____ State: _____ Zip Code_____

- Church Phone*

  (   )_____

- Email: _____ Web Site: _____

- Pastor

  Name: _____

  Address: _____

  Phone: _____ Email: _____

- Date Church was Constituted or Organized: _____

- Number of Current Members: _____

We desire to enter into a covenant relationship with the churches, which
constitute the Berean Missionary Baptist Association, Inc. Our church has
doctrines and practices that agree with the Baptist Faith and Message, and
the goals, doctrines, and practices of the Berean Missionary Baptist
Association, Inc. and its member churches.

Berean Missionary Baptist Association, Inc.

As we have the opportunity, we will participate in the various activities of the Berean Missionary Baptist Association, Inc. and contribute financially to the budget through registration fees, offerings, special offerings, etc.

- Adjourned Session
- Congress of Christian Education
- Annual Session
- Women Auxiliary
- Laymen
- Children & Youth
- Leadership Schools
- Workshops/Seminars

Applications will be considered by the Credentials Committee and presented to the annual meeting for a vote. In some cases, churches applying for membership may be admitted under a "provisional status" for a period of time until a vote is taken for full acceptance.

Please attach to this application the following:

- *A copy of the motions by your church seeking membership in the Berean Missionary Baptist association signed by the pastor and church clerk.*

_____   _____
(Signature) Church Representative   Date

ASSOCIATION USE:

Date Application Received: _____

At: _____

By: _____

Title: _____

Appendix H

Berean Missionary Baptist Association Board of Directors

2023

Executive Board

Pastor Andre Osborne, Moderator

Pastor Thomas Williams, 1st Vice Moderator

Rev. Barbara Simmons, 2nd Vice Moderator

Sis. Carolyn B. Scott, Secretary

Sis. Sheila Arkwright, Clerk

Pastor Joseph Hoze, Treasurer

Women's Auxiliary

Sis. Evelyn Green, President

Rev. Barbara Simmons, 1st Vice President

Min. Brittany Barnes, 2nd Vice President

Min. Tiffany Stewart, Recording Secretary

Congress of Christian Education

Pastor Timothy Sheppard, President

Dea. James Green, Vice President

Sis. Antoinette Ellis Ward, Secretary

Sis. Kathy Morgan, Dean

Dea. Edward Williams, Sr., Director General

Laymen's Auxiliary

Dea. James Green, Interim President

Vice President (vacant)

Secretary (vacant)

Works Cited

Berean Association Executive Board Meeting. Planning Meeting. 31 Aug. 2013.

Berean Association of Churches. 119th Annual Session leaflet.

Berean Missionary Baptist Association, Inc. 109th Annual Session. "The Heavenly Vision: The Mission of the Church." October 14-16, 2009.

"Berean Missionary Baptist Association, Inc. 111th Annual Session." Program Booklet 12 – 14-Oct. 2011).

"Berean Missionary Baptist Association, Inc. 112th Adjourned Session." Program.

"Berean Missionary Baptist Association, Inc. 113th Adjourned Session." Program. 25 Jan. 2014.

"Berean Missionary Baptist Association, Inc. 113th Annual Session." Program. 17-19 Oct.2013.

"Berean Missionary Baptist Association, Inc. 115th Annual Session." Program. 2015.

"Berean Missionary Baptist Association, Inc. 118th Annual Session." Booklet.

"Berean Missionary Baptist Association, Inc. 121st Adjourned Session." Handout.

"Berean Missionary Baptist Association Inc. 121st Adjourned Session." Program, 26 Feb. 2022.

"Berean Missionary Baptist Association, Inc. 122nd Adjourned Session." Program. 22-23 Jan. 2023.

"Berean Missionary Baptist Association, Inc. 122nd Annual Session." Program. 14 -15 Oct. 2022.

"Berean Missionary Association Now in Session," *Savannah Herald*, October 10, 2000.

"Berean Missionary Baptist Association." Pamphlet. 2023.

Berean Senior Saints. Rev. Dr. Carolyn L. Dowse. Report. 118th Annual Session.

"Bereans in the Bible." Thegospelcoalition.org. Accessed 26 Oct. 2022.

Brown, Sr., Matthew Southall. Letter, Revend/Pastor Nathaniel Small, Jr. 12 Sept. 2012.

Christian Leadership School Manual. Revised ed. Sunday School Publishing Board, 2016, p.10.

Congress of Christian Education Pamphlet, 2022. Report. Timothy Sheppard.

"Election." Letter to the Berean Association for 112th Adjourned Session (by Rev. Matthew Southall Brown, Sr.

Flyer. Capers, Robinson, & Daniels Christian Leadership School. 29-31 Jan.2023.

"Greater Works." Purpose Driven Churches of the Berean Missionary Baptist Association, Inc. Booklet, 2016.

"Greater Works." Purpose Driven Churches of the Berean Missionary Baptist Association, Inc. Booklet, 2017.

Green, Evelyn. "Berean Annual Session and Other Info." Received by Emma J Conyers, 22 Oct. 2020.

Green, Evelyn. "Betty West Bio." Received by Emma J. Conyers, 5 Dec. 2022.

Letter of Appreciation. Cover Letter to Reverend George P. Lee, III. By Matthew Southall Brown, Sr., 2008.

Minutes. The Berean Missionary Baptist Association, Inc. 116th Adjourned Session. Carolyn B. Scott.

Minutes. The Berean Missionary Baptist Association, Inc. 117th Annual Session. Carolyn B. Scott 14 Nov. 2022.

Minutes. The Berean Missionary Baptist Association, Inc. 117th Adjourned Session. Carolyn B. Scott. 20-21 Jan, 2018.

Minutes. The Berean Missionary Baptist Association, Inc. 118th Adjourned Session. Carolyn B. Scott. 19 Jan. 2019.

Minutes. The Berean Missionary Baptist Association, Inc. 119th Annual Session. Carolyn B. Scott. 18-19 Oct. 2019).

Minutes. The Berean Missionary Baptist Association, Inc. 119th Adjourned Session. Carolyn B. Scott. 23-24 Feb. 2020.

Minutes. The Berean Missionary Baptist Association, Inc., 121st Annual Session.

"Our Goal." Bereanmba.org. https://www.bereanmba.org/aboutbmba. Accessed 15 Mar. 2023.

Program. "Installation Service for Rev. Dr. Clarence Williams, Jr., Moderator-Elect." 5 Jan. 2013.

Savannah Tribune. 12 Aug. 1899, p. 2, issue 44, vol. XIV.

Savannah Tribune. 11 Aug. 1900, p. 3, issue 44, vol. XV.

Savannah Tribune. 8 Sept. 1900, p. 3, issue 48, vol. XV.

Savannah Tribune. 15 Sept. 1900, p. 3, issue 49, vol. XV.

Savannah Tribune. 20 Jul. 1901, p. 3, issue 41, vol. XVI.

Savannah Tribune. 27 Jul. 1901, p. 3.

Savannah Tribune. 3 Aug. 1901, p. 2, issue 43, vol. XVI.

Savannah Tribune. 26 Jul.1902, p. 3, issue 42, vol. XVII.

Savannah Tribune, Aug.1902.

Savannah Tribune. 2 Aug. 1902, p. 3, issue 43, vol. XVII.

Savannah Tribune. 23 Aug. 1902, issue 46, vol. VXII.

Savannah Tribune. 16 May 1903, issue 44, vol. XV.

Savannah Tribune. 1 Aug. 1903, issue 43, vol. XVIII.

Savannah Tribune. 29 Aug. 1903, p. 2, issue 47, vol. XVII.

Savannah Tribune. 4 Feb. 1905, p.5, issue 18, vol. XX.

Savannah Tribune. 22 Jul. 1905, p.5, issue 42, vol. XX.

Savannah Tribune. 7 Jul. 1906, p.5, issue 40, vol. XXI.

Savannah Tribune. 1 Sept. 1906, p.4, issue 48, vol. XXI.

Savannah Tribune. 27 Jul. 1907, p.4, issue 44, vol. XXII.

Savannah Tribune. 3 Aug. 1907, p. 5, issue 45, vol. XXII.

Savannah Tribune. 17 Aug. 1907, p. 5, issue 47, vol. XXII.

Savannah Tribune. 13 Jun. 1908, p.4, issue 38, vol. XXIII.

Savannah Tribune. 15 Aug. 1908, p. 4, issue 47, vol. XXIII.

Savannah Tribune. 31 Jul. 1909, p. 4, issue 4, vol. XXIV.

Savannah Tribune. 21 Sept. 1912, p. 4, issue 4, vol. XXVIII.

Savannah Tribune. 2 Aug. 1913, p. 1, issue 46, vol. XXVIII.

Savannah Tribune. 9 Aug. 1913, p. 4, issue 47, vol. XXVIII.

Savannah Tribune. 1Aug *1914*, p. 1, issue 45, vol. XXIX.

Savannah Tribune. 15 Aug. 1915, p. 1, issue 47, vol. XXIX.

Savannah Tribune. 24 Jul. 1915, p. 1, issue 44, vol. XXX.

Savannah Tribune. 15 Jul. 1916, p. 1, issue 36, vol. XXXI.

Savannah Tribune. 22 Jul. 1916, p. 1, issue 37, vol. XXXI.

Savannah Tribune. 7 Oct. 1916, p.7, issue 2, vol. XXXII.

Savannah Tribune. 18 May 1918, p.1, issue 37, vol. XXXIII.

Savannah Tribune. 3 Aug. 1918, p. 7, issue 47, vol. XXXIII.

Savannah Tribune. 2 Aug. 1919, p. 6, issue 46, vol. XXXIV.

Savannah Tribune. 31 Jul. 1920, p.1 issue 24, vol. XXXV.

Savannah Tribune. 13 Jul. 1922, p. 1, issue 39, vol. XXXVII.

Savannah Tribune. *30* Nov. 1922, p. 5, issue 7, vol. XXXVII.

Savannah Tribune. 29 Dec. 1922, p.6, issue 11, vol. XXXVIII.

Savannah Tribune. 3 Aug. 1944, front page.

Savannah Tribune. 28 Jan.1945, front page.

Savannah Tribune, 21 June 1945, p. 3.

Savannah Tribune. 5 July 1945, p. 5.

Savannah Tribune. 2 Aug. 1945, p. 3.

Savannah Tribune. 25 Sept. 1947, p. 3.

Savannah Tribune. 4 Mar. 1948, p. 6. *Savannah Tribune.* 2 Aug. 1945.

Savannah Tribune. 23 Sept. 1948, p. 2.

Savannah Tribune. 7 Oct.1948.

Savannah Tribune. 7 Oct. 1948, p. 2.

Savannah Tribune. 7 Oct. 1948, p.6.

Savannah Tribune. 4 Nov. 1948, p. 3.

Savannah Tribune. 9 Feb. 1950, p. 2.

Savannah Tribune 17 Aug. 1950, p. 2.

Savannah Tribune. 12 Jul. 1951, p. 2.

Savannah Tribune. 3 Jan. 1952, p. 6.

Savannah Tribune. 25 Jun. 1953.

Savannah Tribune. 18 Feb. 1954, p. 2.

Savannah Tribune. 9 Feb. 1957, p.3.

Savannah Tribune. 21 Jun. 1958, p. 2.

Savannah Tribune. 11 Jul. 1959, p. 2.

Savannah Tribune. 5 Dec.1959, p. 2.

Savannah Tribune. 23 Jan. 1960.

Savannah Tribune. 30 Jul 2008.

Savannah Tribune. 29 Apr. 2009.

Savannah Tribune. 22 Jul. 2009.

Savannah Tribune. 113th Adjourned Session. 22 Jan. 2014.

Savannah Tribune. 29 Mar. 2017.

Savannah Tribune. 17 Jan. 2018.

Savannah Tribune. 4 Apr. 2018.

Savannah Tribune. 24 Oct 2018.

Savannah Tribune. 6 Mar 2019.

Savannah Tribune. 23 Jul 2019.

Savannah Tribune. 24 Jul 2019.

Savannah Tribune. 14 Jul 2021.

Scriven, Florrie B. Notes. 14 Mar. 2023.

Scriven, Florrie B. Notes, Apr. 2023.

"73rd Session of the Berean Missionary Baptist Association and the 52nd Sessions of the Women's Auxiliary of the Berean Association." Program Booklet. 1972.

Women's Hour Pamphlet. 22 Feb 2022.

Zion Missionary Baptist Association. History Excerpt. Gregory Lattany. Mailed 17 Oct. 2022.

Index

R

S

Weston, W. L. P. 88, 112

White Oak Baptist Church, Monteith,
Georgia 120

White Oak Baptist Church 55,
120, 271

Williams, Jr., Clarence 94, 105, 149,
150, 151, 152, 153, 155, 158,
170, 176, 221, 303

Wilmington Baptist Church 131, 134

Women's Auxiliary xviii, xix, 8, 34,
54, 55, 56, 58, 121, 122, 124,
126, 127, 132, 136, 138, 140,
142, 143, 144, 145, 146, 147,
148, 150, 151, 153, 154, 155,
156, 157, 162, 164, 168, 170,
172, 176, 179, 181, 183, 187,
188, 189, 190, 193, 195, 196,
200, 201, 265, 267, 268, 270,
272, 276, 277, 279, 280, 282,
283, 297, 308

Women's Auxiliary Hour 146,
153, 154

Women's Auxiliary Officers 136,
144, 148, 154, 157, 188, 200

Women's Auxiliary President's
Hour 146

Women's Department 127, 172

World Day of Prayer 197

Y

Young People's Department 147

Youth 29, 32, 42, 44, 51, 58, 79, 81,
93, 107, 137, 139, 144, 147, 151,
152, 153, 154, 156, 157, 159,
162, 167, 171, 173, 174, 176, 177,
178, 185, 186, 189, 192, 193,
194, 195, 196, 197, 198, 200,
234, 235, 265, 272, 273, 275,
276, 277, 281, 292

Youth Day of Prayer 144, 197

Youth Enrichment Sessions 156, 185

Youth Futures Authority (YFA)
153, 159

Youth Hour 139, 151, 154, 189, 192,
193, 194, 276, 281

Z

Zion Hill Baptist Church 77, 161, 163,
194, 197, 198, 231

Zion Hill Missionary Baptist
Church 145

Zion Missionary Baptist Association
110, 111, 112, 113, 149, 277,
282, 308

Note: Churches listed without city and state are located in Savannah, Georgia.

EQUIPPING   EXALTING

Berean
Missionary Baptist Association

Building Healthy Churches

EDIFYING   EVANGELIZING

Printed in the United States
by Baker & Taylor Publisher Services